THE
EVERYDAY
MEAT
GUIDE

THE
EVERYDAY
MEAT
GUIDE

A Neighborhood Butcher's Advice Book

Ray Venezia
with
Chris Peterson

photographs by
ANTONIS ACHILLEOS

CHRONICLE BOOKS
SAN FRANCISCO

TO MY WIFE, DEE DEE, AND OUR THREE CHILDREN,
BARBRA, BOBBY, AND RAYMOND

And with thanks to Carmine Venezia for opening the door to a great education;
to Jane Dystel and Miriam Goderich of Dystel & Goderich Literary Management for helping
make this book a reality; to Joey and Ralph Corrado of Corrado's Market in New Jersey and
Master Purveyors and the Solaz family in New York for providing meat.

Library of Congress Cataloging-in-Publication Data:
Venezia, Ray.
  The everyday meat guide : a neighborhood butcher's advice book / Ray
    Venezia with Chris Peterson.
pages cm
Includes index.
ISBN 978-1-4521-4288-3
1. Meat. I. Peterson, Chris, 1961- II. Title.
  TX373.V46 2016
  641.3'6—dc23

                    2015008240

Manufactured in China

Designed by Vanessa Dina
Illustrations by Amanda Sims
Typesetting by Howie Severson

10 9 8 7 6 5 4

Chronicle Books LLC
680 Second Street
San Francisco, California 94107
www.chroniclebooks.com

INTRODUCTION

I come from a family of butchers three generations deep. I started learning my craft behind the counter at a local meat market, where helping customers meant a lot more than just stocking premium meat and poultry, cut to exacting standards. I was taught it wasn't good enough just to sell a cut of meat, that you always sell the best possible cut for a particular customer and made damn sure that the customer had all the information he or she needed to properly handle, prepare, and cook the cut. I quickly learned never to assume customers knew what they were buying or how to cook it.

When my career path led me to the meat director position at Fairway Markets, in New York, I passed on the mantra of "help the shopper" to everyone who worked for me. I was adamant that my staff never push one cut or another just because they had a lot on hand. I stressed that they needed to listen to the shopper, and then offer advice on the best meat or poultry for that shopper's needs. I taught them that earning customers' trust was a key part of the craft behind the counter.

Along the way, I was invited to offer advice to viewers on programs like *Rachael Ray*, *Fox & Friends*, and *Good Day New York*, where I had the opportunity to pass on valuable lessons to anyone shopping for meat and poultry. The goal was always the same: Help people buy the meat and poultry that delivers the best value for money and the best flavor, given what and how they wanted to cook. Just as I had throughout my career, I used those four-minute TV segments to clear up what can be a very confusing shopping experience.

I'm betting that you know exactly what I'm talking about. If you've stood in front of a packaged-meat case wondering which was the best steak for you, or sliced into a chicken breast that is charred on the outside while still pink on the inside, or passed by a butcher's shop because you were too intimidated to step inside or had no idea what the butcher could do for you, or if you've ever felt like you were paying too much and getting too little when buying meat and poultry, this book is for you.

I've helped thousands of customers identify, buy, and cook the best meat for themselves and their families. The key has always been to anticipate the questions. That can be a challenge sometimes, but the questions shoppers ask have all been asked many times before. That's why I wanted to collect all the answers to those questions in one easy-to-read place—this book.

My goal for every page in this book is that you will shop your meat case with my advice in mind, seeing through my eyes, to pick out the freshest, best-quality meat and poultry. I also help you get the absolute most you can for your grocery budget. And I provide you with plenty of cooking tips, so you can prepare meat and poultry the way that tastes best to you and your family, with no money wasted, no food wasted, and no frustration at the market or in your kitchen.

I've set up the book so that you can just turn to the cut of meat that matters most to you. Have a hankering for a low-cost, high-flavor steak you can grill in a few minutes without a lot of fuss and muss? Turn to page 111. Heard all about how tender and flavorful veal loin is? You'll discover all you need to know on page 094. Want to finally, once and for all, learn the best way to carve your Thanksgiving turkey? Flip to page 137!

I make it that easy for you. Pick a topic, read a few lines, notice the camera icons that tell you which photograph at the back of the book shows the cut (some cuts appear larger in proportion to others to show detail), and you're ready to head out to the store or into your kitchen with confidence. If you aren't sure what cut or particular type of meat you want, a little more background is in order. No worries. In each chapter I've included an in-depth introduction to the meat, along with plenty of boxes that explain key information in more detail.

Navigating a meat case or a butcher shop the smart way is not just a matter of knowing a little bit about the cuts you want and what you could buy. It's also a matter of knowing how different meats are packaged, what different terms actually mean, and how all that affects the best value for you.

LEARNING LABEL LINGO

One of the most valuable lessons you can learn is what a meat-package label is telling you. Reading the label requires a little bit of knowledge, but a close read is essential to make sure that you're buying exactly what you want. You'll find terms on labels that mean next to nothing, but others—required by law—will tell you almost the whole story of what's inside the package.

All packaged meat and poultry sold in a supermarket or other reputable outlet in the United States must be labeled with a United States Department of Agriculture (USDA) inspection label. This tells you the contents are safe for consumption, based on the standards developed and maintained by the USDA. The meat may also be graded (see Making the Grade, page 101). If there is a grade, it will be listed in the middle bar of the USDA shield logo. Beyond the USDA info are label terms that can add to general confusion.

Let's start with the term "natural." This term has been so misused that it has come to mean absolutely nothing. Technically, it describes a product that has no artificial ingredients or color, but the meat may contain residual hormones, antibiotics, processed feed, and other additives and still be considered "natural."

"Organic" is a more legitimate term regulated by the USDA. The USDA Organic shield is an excellent sign of purity. Oddly, the term "organic" alone on a package requires that the contents conform to the same requirements necessary to carry the USDA shield. Producers must go to great expense to secure the USDA Organic inspection and marking. Some producers

008

choose to avoid that expense and instead simply conform to the standards, labeling their products as organic. Store meat departments may buy USDA-certified organic primals (the primary sections of an animal) and break them down into packaged cuts, which produces a less-expensive, fresher product. Because a store's meat department is not USDA-certified, cuts produced this way can only have "organic" on the label and not the USDA Organic shield.

The USDA also regulates the use of the specification "No antibiotics added." Those exact words mean that the producer has provided documentation to show the animal was raised and cared for without antibiotics. Any other version of those words should be considered an unverified claim made by the packager.

"Hormone-free" or "antibiotic-free" means that no growth hormones or antibiotics were present in the slaughtered animal. This isn't to say that antibiotics weren't used at one time or another in the animal's life to treat disease—simply that the drugs were out of the animal's system when it was killed. If you are looking for meat from an animal that was never treated with hormones or antibiotics, look for organic meat.

If you want to shop your conscience, you'll be looking for a "Certified Humane" label. Although not USDA regulated, the term is certified through Humane Farm Animal Care, a nonprofit dedicated to improving the lives of farm animals. The organization has created a set of standards regarding housing, access to open areas to roam, and other requirements, which any certified product must meet.

"Locally grown" or "locally raised" are terms that may not mean what a shopper would reasonably assume. The meat must be slaughtered and processed within 400 mi [644 km] of where it is sold at retail. That said, it can be 400 mi [644 km] in any direction. You may think you are supporting the local economy and dealing with regulations in your state, when the meat could actually be coming from another state altogether.

009

Other terms such as "free-range" and "grass-fed" apply to specific animals and packaging, and you'll find out more about those label terms in the animal-specific sections.

The USDA does not regulate the use of "chemical-free," "residue-free," "residue-tested," or "drug-free" on meat and poultry labels. If these terms are on the label, be leery of what's inside.

One last word about labels: A somewhat controversial term right now is **Country of Origin Labeling (COOL)**. The USDA currently mandates that either the individual labels on packages of meat or the case in which they are sold must state the country in which the animal was raised, even if it was slaughtered in the United States. The underlying idea is that consumers should be able to determine the standards by which the animal was raised. Unfortunately there's a lot of wiggle room in the term. Plus, quality, guidelines, and regulations for meat inspections vary widely from state to state, let alone from country to country. The meat industry remains involved in a court battle to eliminate COOL requirements.

MEAT CUTS LINGO

Beyond the issues involved with selecting, buying, and cooking specific cuts, there are general terms that you'll find useful to know before you head out to the supermarket or to your local butcher shop. These are often misunderstood.

Roast. Not all roasts are created equal. When most people say "roast" they are talking about a large piece of meat cooked, uncovered, in the oven using high-temperature dry heat. Unfortunately, not every cut with "roast" on the label fits the bill. **Boneless chuck roast, shoulder roast, bottom round,** and **rump roast** are some of the most common and affordable of all the roast cuts for beef. But these should not be cooked in high-temperature dry heat. They should be cooked in pots, with about 4 cups [960 ml] of liquid for slow, penetrating cooking. Cooked correctly, these cuts will come out flavorful and tender and are an economical way to feed a group.

010

Steak. Just because you see the word "steak" on the label of a package of beef is no guarantee that what you're getting is really steak. Most shoppers think steak is a piece of meat with a strong beef flavor, a cut perfectly suited to grilling. Well, in the meat industry, professionals use the word to describe any cut sliced into individual-serving sizes. Cuts like **shoulder steaks, flat iron steaks,** and **chuck steaks** will not grill well even though they may be sliced thin. They need tenderizing; moist, low-temperature cooking; or a long bath in an acidic marinade to become tender. True beef steak cuts come from the rib section, back through the loin of the animal. These cuts will be leaner than steak cuts from the chuck (the front of the animal) and have a stronger beef flavor. The meat will also stand up to the intense heat of grilling.

011

Chop. For pork, lamb, and veal, chops are the equivalent of beef steaks. When is a chop not a chop? When the word "end" is on the label, as in **rib end chop** and **loin end chop.** These are not the types of chops that you throw on the grill, and neither is a **shoulder chop.** These cuts are better suited for moist, low-temperature cooking (rib end or shoulder chops) or roasting (loin end). If you're looking to grill chops, you'll want either **center-cut chops,** or **rib** or **loin chops.**

Knowing what meat-cut terms mean is just the first step in getting the best value for your money at a meat case or a butcher's counter. How you handle the meat and poultry you buy is just as important.

BEYOND THE LABEL

What you see through the plastic can tell you a lot, because the difference between a fresh and not-so-fresh cut of meat is plain to see. Regardless of the cut, you don't want to see a lot of moisture in a package. Ideally, there should be no liquid pooling in the package. The plastic should always be wrapped tightly—air is the enemy of fresh meat and poultry—and the plastic should be completely clear, not fogged.

Once you bring your meat home, it's wise to freeze it if you don't intend to use it within 24 hours. How long a piece of meat will stand up to freezing, and the best way to thaw a cut, is explained in detail in the chapters that follow.

PRESERVING MOISTURE AND FLAVOR

Different types of meat, and different cuts, vary in how much moisture they retain during cooking. And where moisture goes, flavor is sure to follow. Marinades and rubs flavor the meat or poultry. Brines are essentially saltwater baths and are meant primarily to preserve moistness during cooking. They impart a salty taste, while rubs and marinades add more complex flavors. You'll find suggestions for how keep your meat moist in the information about individual cuts in each chapter.

KNIFE KNOW-HOW

Working with meat and poultry requires some basic kitchen cutlery. The right knives can make anything you do in the kitchen a lot easier. I have two rules about kitchen knives: They don't have to cost a fortune, and you only need two basic knives for working with meat.

012

8- to 10-in [20- to 25-cm] slicing knife. This is not a traditional chef's knife; it has a narrower blade that curves up slightly at the end. Buy one with a blade thick enough to resist bending and stand up to several sharpenings. Razor-thin knives that have a lot of bend can be dangerous to work with because they can flex and quickly slice a hand or digit that is near the meat. Handles come in different lengths and widths. Choose one that is comfortable in your hand. It should have a slight lip on the front, where the blade meets the handle, to keep your hand from sliding off the handle and onto the blade. I prefer softer wooden handles to hard plastic.

6- to 7-in [15- to 17-cm] boning knife. This knife must also be thick enough for regular sharpening and should be weighty and substantial enough to hold up to repeated collisions with bone and cutting boards.

You might want to consider adding these knives:

Carving knife. You can buy a carving knife as part of any knife set or separately. Buy a high-quality model because you'll probably only be using it on special occasions when you need to carve a bird or a big cut of meat (such as a ham). However, I use my slicing knife for this purpose, and so can you.

Chef's knife. Admittedly, this can be more comfortable for chopping vegetables than a slicing knife is, so I understand why a lot of cooks like to add one to their kitchen tools. Buy a heavy-bladed 10-in [25-cm] chef's knife for all-around kitchen duty.

013

Knowing how to keep your knives sharp is also essential for success. Ripping a piece of meat instead of cutting it is a bad start to any recipe. Knife sharpness is also a safety issue—a vast number of kitchen knife accidents happen because a knife is dull. In fact, among butchers there is a saying, "You get cut by a dull knife, not a sharp one." Almost every store-bought kitchen knife set comes with a steel, but *a steel will not sharpen the blade*—it just straightens the edge of the blade, which turns every time the blade hits the cutting board, helping to hold the edge between sharpenings. Unless you understand how to sharpen a knife, have a professional sharpen your kitchen knives for you with a whetstone.

MEAT AND POULTRY COOKING TEMPERATURES

No matter which protein you plan to cook, use a quality, instant-read thermometer to check internal temperature for doneness. I know that there are many homespun ways to check a piece of meat's doneness, but the most reliable and best way is to take an accurate reading of the internal temperature. The temperatures in the chart opposite include the official USDA recommendations (except where otherwise noted). When choosing a doneness temperature, keep in mind that the best trick to cooking succulent meat is to retain as much moisture as possible during cooking. That moisture equals flavor and tenderness, which is why I recommend cooking most cuts medium-rare. The listings throughout the book often mention my preferences for doneness; refer back to this chart for exact temperatures.

014

COOKING TEMPERATURES

All Meat
Ground: 160°F [71°C]

Poultry
All cuts: 165°F [74°C]

Pork Steaks, Roasts, and Chops:

Medium-rare 145°F [63°C] + 2 minutes rest*

Medium 150°F [66°C]*

Medium-well—No recommendation

Well 160°F [71°C]*

Lamb, Veal, and Beef Steaks, Roasts, and Chops:

Rare 125° to 130°F [52° to 54°C] + 3 to 5 minutes rest*

Medium-rare 145°F [63°C] + 3 to 5 minutes rest*

Medium 160°F [71°C] + 3 to 5 minutes rest*

Medium-well—No recommendation

Well—No recommendation

* This is a professional recommendation. (There is no recommendation from the USDA for this specific doneness.)

015

POULTRY

Having stocked more packaged-poultry displays than I can count, I am still amazed by the diversity of cuts that producers manage to get from what are pretty simple animals. Pick the right cut, and you'll enjoy a protein-rich, low-fat meal with mild to medium flavor. Choose the wrong one, and you could easily end up with a dried-out, tasteless dinner.

When I started out, all the chicken was delivered to the store packed in ice in wooden crates. If you were shopping where I worked, you knew you were getting fresh poultry, cut professionally. I wasn't such a fan on the other side of the counter. Cutting and packaging chicken was the coldest, wettest, most unpleasant work you could do, and most butchers hated processing the chicken. So as an apprentice, I was volunteered to do the chicken. It certainly helped me build up hand strength and cutting speed. The only way I was going to get to work on the meat was to get through that chicken first.

Unfortunately, things are a little different these days. Most of the people behind the meat counter in supermarkets don't have much of a say about what goes into the packages on display. The truth is, 80 to 90 percent of the chicken delivered to supermarkets is prepackaged. That's why it's more important than ever for the consumer to be able to "read" the package. Not just the label but the package itself. You'll need to do a little detective work to get the best poultry for your grocery budget.

Whole turkeys, whole chickens, and specialty game birds are a different matter. It's not so much about packaging but about the bird itself. Size and how the bird was raised are going to be the most important considerations. In the case of turkeys, especially, you're going to want to go the extra mile to find and buy quality birds, because they are usually special-occasion purchases.

When I'm shopping for poultry to feed my family, I always look for the words "free-range," "vegetarian-fed," or "pasture-raised" on the label. These terms indicate that the bird was fed a mostly or completely natural diet, won't be filled with additives, and was healthier to begin with. "Cage-free" is a USDA term that describes poultry that did not live in cages and had unlimited access to food and water. However, keep in mind that just because the birds weren't caged, doesn't mean they were raised in sanitary or humane conditions. There's a lot to know about these terms.

Free-range: The standard for free-range birds is that the flock be provided with shelter in a building or covered area with unlimited access to food and fresh water, and "continuous access" to outdoors. This has nothing to do with what the birds are fed, and just

017

because chickens have access does not mean they use it. It's not uncommon to pass a chicken farm and see all the chickens huddled together inside, rather than running around outside. However, in general, any free-range bird is going to be tastier and healthier than an industrial bird that was housed in what are often unhealthful and cramped conditions. "Free-range" from an organic farm usually means that the chicken had the run of a large pen or may have even been let loose for most of the day. When a bigger producer labels bird parts "free-range," they often mean it was given a little outdoor time in a pen. Look for "free-range" coupled with "vegetarian-fed" on the label. This combination ensures a healthier, better-tasting bird.

Pasture-raised: This is a step beyond free-range, meaning that the birds were actually given an area of pasture in which to run free (and eat a more varied diet, including protein-rich insects). Because of the variables involved in pasture-raised systems, the USDA has not developed a definition for "pasture-raised." That, in my opinion, leaves too much wiggle room for the producers and makes this term a less-powerful guide for shoppers than it should be.

Cage-free: This term means the birds were able to roam a building or an enclosed area with unlimited access to food and fresh water. But it doesn't mean the building was especially clean, well lit, or appropriately ventilated.

Organic: When the word "organic" appears on a poultry label, it means that no chemicals were introduced into the bird—through its feed, veterinary treatments, the environment, or processing. Basically everything from what it ate to the cleaning products used around the chickens would meet the requirements for a Certified Organic shield. Poultry that could qualify as USDA Organic but that are packaged in a non-USDA-certified plant can carry only the word "organic" on the label. These birds will be a little less expensive than Certified Organic poultry, but they are the same high-quality product.

Raised responsibly: This is as much about culture and beliefs as it is about the health of the bird. Responsible husbandry involves raising poultry and other farm animals in a humane way—with a good diet, a reasonable amount of space, and as stress-free an existence as can be realistically provided. The birds are also slaughtered in the most humane way possible. This all contributes to poultry that tastes better and is easier on the consumer's conscience. The only way to know for sure is to see the Certified Humane logo on the package.

POULTRY TYPES AND SIZES

019

Another important aspect of buying poultry is knowing the various kinds of birds you'll find on sale. Here's what wise shoppers should know (listed in order of most commonly to least commonly purchased).

Broiler or fryer: Any chicken 7 to 9 weeks old and weighing from 2½ to 4½ lb [1.2 to 2 kg] can be called a broiler or fryer. The meat is tender, but the bird lacks moisturizing and flavoring fat, which is why these chickens are best for broiling, frying, or braising.

Roaster: A chicken, 8 to 12 weeks and weighing 5 to 7 lb [2.3 to 3.2 kg] is ideal for oven roasting or cooking on a rotisserie.

Stewing hen: Also called **fowl,** this is a mature laying hen, 1 to 1½ years old and weighing more than 4 lb [1.8 kg]—sometimes as much as 7 lb [3.2 kg]. Although more flavorful, the meat in an older chicken tends to be a bit tougher and stringier, which is why they are best used for stews.

Capon: A young male chicken, less than 4 months old, which has been castrated. As males, they have more fat and more meat than female chickens, but the process and aging necessary for maximum flavor makes capons a rare find these days. They aren't supplied by industrial producers, so you're most likely to come across a capon in a food co-op or an organic grocery store that buys local.

Poussin: A young chicken less than 1 month old, usually weighing under 1 lb [455 g]. That's why it is sometimes called "spring chicken." It is expensive, but the meat is very tender, the flavor is light and delicate, and the bird has very little fat. Like capons, poussins are fairly hard to find. Chefs commonly substitute Rock Cornish game hens.

Rock Cornish game hen: The Cornish game hen is just a small, young broiler less than 5 weeks old and weighing 1 to 2 lb [455 to 910 g]. Most of the birds raised for meat in the United States today are from the Cornish and White Rock breeds. The Cornish breed is British and the White Rock was developed in New England, where the term "Rock Cornish game hen" comes from.

Poulet Rouge chicken: A heritage breed known for its flavor and high quality. The chicken matures about 4 weeks later than other breeds (12 versus 8 weeks). It is difficult to find and expensive, but worth the effort and price. This was the chicken of choice before crossbreeding took over in the pursuit of plumper breasts with more white meat on chickens that could be matured faster. The Poulet Rouge has a thinner, more elongated breast and longer legs, giving it more dark meat than conventional chickens. But make no mistake, this is the most flavorful chicken you will ever taste.

Broiler or fryer duckling: This is a young duck, usually less than 8 weeks old, of either sex. The ducklings range in weight from 3 to 6 lb [1.4 to 2.7 kg]. Like their chicken counterparts, they are less flavorful and fatty than adult versions and are best used for broiling or frying.

DETERMINING FRESHNESS

When you shop for packaged poultry, start with the store label on the front of the package. The label is required by law to list the type and cut of poultry. Although there is no rule that the package must say "fresh," it does have to indicate whether the poultry was previously frozen. The label must also include the sell-by date. In the case of prepackaged chicken, the producer usually provides that date—which allows the store to hold the producer responsible for freshness. Let's be clear, though: A sell-by or use-by date is a rec-ommended *outer limit* for spoilage. It's there to ensure that nobody sells, buys, or cooks spoiled poultry. But it's not a real indicator of freshness. For that, you'll have to closely examine the package and find the date from the plant. It's usually stamped right on the plastic—along the bottom at the back, or sometimes along the side on the front—so it may be a little hard to read. In some cases, such as for repackaged poultry, there may be only the sell-by date, so you'll have to go by that. Shop for packages with at least 7 to 10 days until the producer's sell-by date, or 3 to 4 days until the store's label date. The more days between producer's sell-by date and the pack-aging date, if there is one, the better.

021

You'll also want to determine the quality of the poultry. Grades are the best way to do that. Unfortunately, although the USDA must inspect chickens, grading them is optional.

Any packaged raw poultry you buy should be clearly stamped "Inspected for wholesomeness by U.S. Department of Agriculture." This indicates the poultry has been inspected and is free from visible signs of disease. To receive a **Grade A** stamp, the poultry has to meet higher standards. It must have a plump, meaty body and clean skin. It will be free of bruises, broken bones, feathers, cuts, and discoloration. But before you judge a producer whose products don't carry a grade, understand that producers have to

pay to have their poultry graded. This is one more thing that drives up the price of raising antibiotic- and hormone-free birds. It's why most organic poultry isn't labeled with a grade.

You can use your eyes to determine the quality of packaged poultry. Look at the front of the package, move it around, and view it at different angles. Here's what you *don't* want to see: significant amounts of juice, blood, or liquid of any kind pooled inside the package. Liquid is a sign that moisture is coming out of the cut as it ages, and that the cut has been in the package awhile, or has been in and out of refrigeration. Or the liquid can be an indication that the cut was previously frozen. The skin is another "tell." Translucent skin indicates the bird *isn't* fresh. If you can see the meat through the skin, even if the package is dry, don't buy that package.

Here's what you're looking for in an ideal package of poultry:

- A label listing a sell-by date with at least 2 days to go before expiration.

- A **USDA Grade A** stamp (keeping in mind that smaller producers may not go to the expense of having their product graded).

- Skin color that is somewhere between creamy white and deep corn yellow, and well dimpled.

022

UNDERSTANDING
SERVING PORTIONS FOR CHICKEN

When poultry night comes around, here's what you'll need to satisfy a family of two adults and two children.

1 broiler: 3 to 3½ lb [1.4 to 1.6 kg]. There will be leftovers.

2 whole chicken breasts or 4 chicken breast halves, bone-in or boneless: If you buy bone-in breasts, the meat will shrink less—you might easily get enough out of larger breasts to feed five to six people.

5 or 6 thighs, bone-in or boneless: Thigh meat is denser than breast meat, so you can use a little less to satisfy the same appetite.

3 whole legs (airline cut): Good for roasting, grilling, or slow cooking.

1½ lb [680 g] ground turkey or chicken: For burgers. Used in other dishes, this will depend on the amount of other ingredients in the recipe.

1 turkey breast, bone-in or boneless: Buy 4 lb [1.8 kg] for bone-in and 3 lb [1.4 kg] for boneless.

023

- A clean, tightly wrapped package, with no fluid and no dried stains from fluid. No fluid leaking out means no air getting in.
- A local source. The closer, the better. The less distance the bird has to travel to the slaughterhouse, the less stressed it becomes. Local poultry also travels less time to the market, so it's going to be fresher than industrial birds.

BONE-IN OR NOT?

One of the big questions running through most shoppers' minds when they're standing in front of the poultry case looking at packaged cuts is, "Should I buy bone-in or not?" Larger cuts, such as whole breasts, benefit from a bone. Cook a whole breast with the bone in, and it will shrink less, stay juicier, and come off that bone super-easy when you have it on the cutting board. Braise it, and it will fall off the bone on its own. Because smaller cuts cook quickly, they don't benefit from a bone.

HOW TO STORE AND HANDLE POULTRY

Poultry can be bought in bulk—for example, when it's on sale—and frozen. Freeze poultry the same day you buy it, if you're not going to use it immediately. As I always tell customers, you can only thaw fresh chicken if that's what you put in the freezer in the first place. And just to be clear, for those who think freezing stops bacterial growth—it doesn't. It just slows it way down. And that's a reason to freeze only fresh poultry, in which bacteria hasn't yet gotten the chance to proliferate.

To freeze poultry parts properly, remove them from the store packaging and wrap them tightly in freezer paper, waxed side facing the meat, and put them inside a resealable plastic freezer bag. Squeeze all the air out of the bag before you seal it. Write the date, name of cut, and number of pieces or weight on the package; you don't want to be playing the guessing game when you're pulling out dinner on a weeknight. Believe it or not, if you prepare poultry for freezing in this way, it can last 4 to 6 months in the freezer.

When you're ready to cook, thaw the cuts in the refrigerator just enough so that the outside softens—not all the way. If you let it defrost until moisture starts to run out, the poultry can wind up tough and bland.

Any time you handle poultry, rinse and pat it dry before using (making sure not to splash out of the sink when rinsing). Make sure that anything that comes into contact with the poultry—knives, cutting boards, the countertop, and your hands—spends some quality time in hot, sudsy water. Better yet, add a few drops of bleach to the water when cleaning everything—it's great for killing the bacteria that can hide in chop lines, handle seams, and other nooks and crannies.

Duck, Duck, Goose

Duck and geese are not everyday poultry purchases, but they can make a holiday or any special occasion more festive. A duck or a goose can be an incredible alternative to a turkey. The heavy fats and oils in these birds make the meat dense and rich with flavor, and make the birds perfect for roasting. The richness of the meat also means you need less to feed a crowd than you would a turkey or chicken. A 4-lb [1.8-kg] duck or goose will feed four to six people.

What to look for: The low demand for duck and geese means that they have to be preserved prior to sale. That's why most are sold vacuum-packed and frozen. That's okay. The strong flavors in the meat survive freezing well. And, quite frankly, some less-than-scrupulous sellers will allow frozen birds to thaw and then sell those birds as fresh. So I always advise people to buy frozen ducks or geese. Feel along the bottom of a vacuum-sealed frozen bird. The wrap should be tight, with no air pockets. Looseness or puffing is a sign that the vacuum seal has failed. Frozen correctly with a tight vacuum seal, a duck or goose can last 6 to 8 months in the freezer.

How to cook it: Thaw a duck or goose to room temperature before cooking (following the same procedure you would use for a turkey, see page 029). Roast the bird as you would a turkey, on a roasting rack or on carrots to keep the bird up and out of its own juices. To make the skin pleasingly brown and satisfyingly crispy, lightly prick the skin of the breast in several places with a pin. Be careful to just penetrate the surface of the skin, not the meat below. This allows the oils that come out during cooking to drain over the outside of the bird, basting it as it cooks.

Cook the bird in an oven preheated to 425°F [220°C], lowering the temperature to 350°F [180°C] when you put the bird in. Roast for 25 minutes per 1 lb [455 g] (as with chicken and turkey, the internal temp should reach 165°F [74°C]). Remove the bird and let it sit for 10 to 15 minutes before carving.

USING THE EXTRAS

The internal organs of any whole bird, including the neck, heart, liver, kidney, and gizzards, are called the giblets. These are collected by the producer in a plastic bag and stashed in the body cavity. A lot of people simply throw these extras out or give them to the family pet. But make no mistake, they are delicacies.

Because the livers are a popular item and are considered the crown jewel of the giblets, they are often not included in the package. You can, however, purchase them separately. Poultry livers are nutritious and taste great made into a paté or fried with onions. Livers are also inexpensive, compared with the cost of the rest of the bird. Fried gizzards are a delicacy in some parts of the world, but I recommend using them with the neck to add flavor to stocks, soups, or stuffing. They make an incredible gravy, which will put any turkey meal over the top.

Ground Poultry (not pictured)

Ground chicken and turkey are low-fat substitutes for ground beef, and have their own wonderfully light flavor. Not only will you be getting quality protein, you'll be getting it at a bargain price.

There are two types of ground poultry: noodle grind and coarse ground. Noodle grind is the most common. If you don't clearly see the individual strands, chances are that the meat has gotten too warm, has been in the package too long, or has been handled by a lot of customers and is starting to break down. The meat is not necessarily bad, but the flavor is going to be blander than it would be in a fresher package. Coarse-ground poultry is, just as you might imagine by the name, processed through a plate with larger holes, so that the end product is chunkier. Unlike noodle-grind poultry, you'll be able to see the fat in the pieces quite clearly. The bigger pieces mean that less natural juice is lost during processing, and coarse-ground poultry retains more flavor. This makes it ideal for sausage, chili, or stuffing.

What to look for: Buy fresh store-ground poultry, or prepackaged with at least 5 days to go before the label's expiration date. You should be able to clearly see the strands of meat. Color should be consistent throughout. Because ground poultry warms up so quickly, get it home and into the refrigerator or freezer as fast as possible. If the store gives you a choice of paper or plastic bags, the cold will hold better in paper. Keep in mind that any ground meat is more perishable than a whole cut, and ground poultry is the most perishable of all ground meats. Freeze it if you're not using it the day you buy it.

How to cook it: No matter what grind you choose, ground poultry is extremely versatile. It's like a blank canvas in the kitchen— especially for burgers. When using it in burgers, for instance, add steak sauce for a rich poultry burger that mimics the flavor of beef. Or mix your favorite chopped veggies into ground chicken for a healthful, hearty burger that will satisfy any appetite. Add seasonings

★
Ray's ADVICE

When you shop, put your ground poultry (or any ground meat, for that matter) in your basket last, right before you check out. This simple practice will ensure that you get home with the freshest ground poultry for your family.

to ground poultry straight from the refrigerator—it will be easier to work with. Freeze poultry burgers until you're ready to grill them. Putting burgers on the grill frozen will keep them from falling apart and sticking. Chili is one of my favorite ways to use ground turkey, because the meat just soaks up all the flavors in the mix.

Whole Chicken

001

If you're like me, you want to stretch your food budget as far as possible. There are few better ways to do that than with a whole chicken. I love whole chickens for cooking, and I've always felt that they are underused in the kitchen.

What to look for: Look for a 3- to 3½-lb [1.4- to 1.6-kg] chicken. The bones are roughly the same as in a smaller bird, but the meat-to-bone ratio is higher. That means you're getting a lot more delicious meat for the money. However, don't go too big. A chicken gets bigger as it ages, and older birds are tougher because they've used their muscles more. So stay under 4 lb [1.8 kg], unless you're buying a roaster, which usually ranges from 5 to 7 lb [2.3 to 3.2 kg].

A whole chicken is also going to leave you with some wonderful scraps for soups and stocks. That's why it's hard to beat a whole bird in the value-for-money department.

How to cook it: Whole chicken is great roasted. Coat it with a rub made from olive oil, garlic, and rosemary and roast it breast-side up in the oven at 425°F [220°C] for 10 to 15 minutes, then lower the heat to 375°F [190°C] and cook for 10 minutes per 1 lb [455 g]. Let the chicken sit for 15 minutes before slicing. Grill a whole chicken on a rotisserie or—my preference—split it in half down the middle and cook it on a grill. Don't bother cutting chicken that comes off the grill—pull it off the bones. Pulled chicken is flat-out delicious.

028

002

Whole Turkey

A whole turkey is something else altogether. Given how expensive a turkey can be, you'll want to make sure that you buy the right size for your crowd and cook it perfectly so that you can make good use of any leftovers.

Fresh or frozen? That's the big decision when it comes to buying a whole turkey. Some people order fresh, thinking that the bird was killed just a few days before. But fresh just means never frozen. The turkeys are still vacuum-packed and chilled well ahead to keep up with holiday demand and hold up better when shipped. Because there's no thawing necessary with a fresh turkey, you'll pay a premium for one. That's why most shoppers buy frozen turkeys. I always buy fresh turkeys myself, because quality is easier to deter-mine and they are so much easier to prepare and cook.

However, don't be fooled when shopping ahead of the holiday if someone tells you that for the freshest bird, buy the bird closer to the actual holiday. "Fresh" turkeys are being vacuum-packed while you are having that conversation. If you have the room, buy your turkey ahead of the crowds and avoid all the handling that turkeys experience in the case. Leave it packaged, and put it in the back of the refrigerator or in a cooler kept chilled until you are ready to cook it (up until the sell-by date). Then wash and rinse the cavity with warm salt water to prepare it for cooking.

Thawing a big frozen turkey is a long process—it takes hours and sometimes days. You can thaw the bird in a shallow pan in the refrigerator. Or, if you don't have room, thaw it in a sink full of cold water (or in any big container, such as a large cooler). Change the water every half hour and weigh the turkey down to make sure it stays submerged. Thawing the turkey in water will take 1 hour for every 2 lb [910 g]. If you have the room, and water conservation is not an issue where you live, leave the water running over the turkey. This will cut the thawing time in half. Thawing a turkey in the refrigerator usually takes 24 hours for every 5 lb [2.3 kg]. No matter how you thaw the bird, leave it in its original packaging until you're ready to cook it. Then remove the wrapping and rinse the cavity with warm salt water if you wish.

029

What to look for: When buying a turkey, I figure 1 lb [455 g] per person, plus 6 to 7 lb [2.7 to 3.2 kg] extra. Hens taste best, and the upper limit for a hen is 20 lb [9 kg]. Any bird larger than that is a tom (male). It's wiser to buy a smaller turkey and supplement as necessary with a turkey breast or boneless turkey breast roast. A boneless turkey breast roast will give you the additional white meat that most people prefer, in a form that is easy to slice. Leftovers? No problem. Sliced turkey breast makes fantastic sandwiches. I know that some people opt for two smaller birds rather than one large one, but I strongly advise against that. You'll inevitably wind up with more wings and drumsticks and a lot of leftovers that, a week later, just get thrown out.

I would never buy precooked turkey. Frankly, if time is that important to you, eat at a restaurant. You can save a little time by buying a cleaned and preseasoned bird, ready to just pop in the oven.

How to cook it: Place the turkey breast-side up in a roasting pan with a rack. Stuck without a rack for your roasting pan? That's okay. Just sit the turkey on six red potato halves spaced evenly across the bottom of the pan, cut-side down. Sit the bird on top of them to

Ray's ADVICE

Always check vacuum-packed turkeys before buying. Run your hand along the underside seam. Check for any air pockets. If it is tight against the back of the turkey, there is a good seal and little chance that air has gotten in and sped up bacterial growth.

030

ABOUT BRINING

Back in the day (and I mean hundreds of years ago), brining was just another way to preserve meat and poultry. Brining uses salt to lock in flavor and moisture, while stopping microbial growth. But as far as a turkey (or even a chicken) goes, the process is all about moisturizing. You can buy brined turkeys, but it's a simple process to do yourself at home, and you can add flavorings to the brine to suit your own preferences.

Start with the container. You'll find brining bags widely available, especially around the holidays. These are handy, easy to use, and limit the amount of brine you'll need. But depending on the size of the turkey and the size of your refrigerator, you may need to use a container, such as a 5-gl [19-L] pail or a large, tailgate-worthy, watertight cooler. Either way, you'll need to keep the turkey cool and submerged while it soaks in the brine. Like all things turkey, you'll need time: plan on 1 hour of brining time for each 1 lb [455 g] of turkey. Heads up though—make sure the turkey you're using hasn't already been brined or preserved, or you could wind up with a bird too salty to eat. Kosher turkeys, for instance, are always sold brined.

1. Dissolve 1 cup [160 g] kosher salt and ¾ cup [150 g] granulated sugar in 2 to 3 cups [480 to 720 ml] of hot water, for each 1 gl [3.8 L] of brine. Mix into 8 to 10 cups [2 to 2.4 L] of cool water, and add flavoring spices as desired. Chili powder, garlic salt, onion powder, and cumin are all good choices.

2. Submerge the turkey, using weights as necessary to ensure it doesn't float. The brine should cover the bird. Add ice to keep the bird cool if you aren't chilling the container in your refrigerator.

3. Remove the turkey and discard the brine. Rinse the turkey thoroughly inside and out and pat dry. You're ready to cook your bird!

031

ensure proper heat and air circulation and add 2 to 4 cups [480 to 960 ml] of broth or warm water if you're concerned that the juices might burn on the bottom of the pan.

Preheat the oven to 475°F [240°C]. Cover the turkey with a foil tent and slide it into the oven. After 15 minutes, lower the temperature to 325°F [165°C]. Give it about 12 minutes per 1 lb [455 g] total cooking time. Remove the foil tent for the last hour of cooking and baste for that nice golden brown color. You can use an instant-read thermometer if you have one; if not, most turkeys come with a pop-up timer. If the thermometer reads 165°F [74°C], you're done. Another way to check doneness is to move the leg away from the body slightly. If the juices run clear, the turkey is done.

Whole Leg (also known as Airline Cut)

003

As much as I'm not a fan of the drumstick, you can get good value by buying whole legs—which are the thigh and drumstick together—what chefs call the **airline cut** (because they were less expensive and consequently used in the early days of airline meals). This cut costs less than buying the thigh or drumstick separately. The whole leg is perfectly sized to feed one person and is ideal for many different cooking methods, including roasting, grilling, and even slow cooking. The strong flavor of the thigh makes the whole cut delicious.

032

What to look for: You can't discuss the whole leg without talking about the quartered chicken leg, which is the lowest-priced cut you'll find in the poultry case (if you can find it). It is roughly the same cut as a whole leg, but a section of the back remains attached to the cut. The back piece adds flavor, but it also adds bone. Although the price is lower, the weight of the extra bone means that you're actually paying the same price for the meat in a quartered chicken leg as you would for the meat in a whole leg. Aside from the lower price, the advantage of a quartered chicken leg is that the bone will ensure the meat shrinks less and retains more flavor. In either case, check the exposed bone; it should be white, not gray. Make sure the bone in the drumstick is not broken.

How to cook it: I've got a secret recipe that I'll give you for absolutely delicious whole legs. It's my barbecue-style slow-cooker chicken. You'll need 6 quartered whole legs; 1 cup [360 g] honey; one 18-oz [510-ml] bottle of your favorite barbecue sauce; and 6 garlic cloves, sliced. Season the legs with salt and pepper and combine them with the honey, barbecue sauce, and garlic in a slow cooker. Cook on low for 5 to 6 hours. It will feed four to six people without a lot of cleanup.

Drumstick

004

The drumstick has become the dinosaur of chicken parts. It is not as meaty as it looks, especially with the cartilage-like bone running through it. It's really no surprise that when chicken nuggets came along, they became the go-to item for kids' dinners and snacks, supplanting the drumstick.

What to look for: The drumstick's main selling point is the built-in handle. But that's not much of a selling point to me, and I find it the least valuable of all the poultry parts. If you're set on drumsticks for dinner, feel the package to make sure the bone running through the drumstick is not broken. Then look at the exposed bone on both ends. The bone should be white and shiny; a grayish tinge is the sign of drumsticks that have been around too long.

How to cook it: The bone running through the drumstick radiates heat from inside, which is why the drumstick cooks faster than any other part. You can roast drumsticks in a pan with potatoes and veggies or soak them in your favorite marinade and grill them (turn the drumsticks several times to ensure even cooking on all sides). However, I feel the best way to prepare drumsticks is breaded and fried. When the breading hits the hot oil it creates a crust that traps juices inside, preventing the meat from shrinking and keeping the drumstick moist and flavorful.

033

Thigh

005

Chicken thighs are so flavorful that it doesn't matter if the bone is in or not. If you accidentally buy bone-in thighs, don't take the bone out until after they are cooked. Not only will you get a little more flavor and slightly less shrinkage, but the bone will pretty much fall out after cooking, and you won't lose the meat that would otherwise stick to it.

What to look for: Boneless thighs are my favorite; they are the undiscovered treasures of the poultry case. The dark meat of the thigh is denser and more saturated with natural fat and oils than breast meat is, giving the thigh meat its rich flavor and juiciness. These natural tenderizers make this cut incredibly versatile and perfect for any kind of cooking. The thighs are also cheaper than most other cuts. Here's another thing about thighs—kids love them. There's something about smaller cuts that makes kids more comfortable with a thigh on the plate than a big breast. Stock up on thighs when they go on sale, because they freeze well.

How to cook it: Boneless chicken thighs were made to be grilled. Here's what I do: Soak wooden skewers in water for 1 hour or up to overnight. Then thread one skewer through the top of each thigh and a second skewer through the bottom (this stabilizes the thighs on the grill), putting four to five thighs on the two skewers. All the rich, delicious meat needs is a quick drizzle of vegetable oil and a generous seasoning of kosher salt and freshly ground pepper and they'll grill up great. Just keep in mind that because the meat is denser, thighs take longer to cook than chicken breasts. Expect to grill them 7 to 10 minutes per side.

034

Breast

006

Breasts are the most popular poultry cut by a wide margin, and the most common form sold are breast halves. They cook quickly, the meat soaks up flavors like a sponge, and finicky eaters have no problem with them. The challenge with any cut of chicken breast is to keep it from drying out and losing its flavor during cooking. The best-tasting breast will come from a medium chicken. Not only does a chicken get bigger as it gets older, it gets fatter as well. That

Ray's ADVICE

When cooking chicken, one sign that it is done is that the juices run clear when pierced with the tip of a sharp knife. If the juices have even the slightest red tinge, the meat is not fully cooked.

adds flavor to the breast meat. But the breast meat in larger chickens can be tough. That's why I choose medium-size chicken breasts; they yield the best overall satisfaction.

Whole breast: The whole breast is the crown jewel of all the breast cuts. As with other bone-in cuts, the bone keeps the meat moist. It starts with more natural moisture and will retain more juice and flavor during cooking than any other breast cut. In fact, this is the only type of breast I will grill. Whole chicken breasts are a way to have all white meat and still feed a lot of people. The standard serving is 12 oz [340 g] per person. One full 2- to 2½-lb [910-g to 1.2-kg] chicken breast feeds at least two people.

035

Split breast: This barbecue staple is a whole breast that has been cut down the middle. Mass production makes this the worst pre-packaged chicken item in the case. The breasts are often mis-cut, with more bone on one side than the other or with other defects. They are also packaged one on top of another (shingled), making it hard to inspect them. I'd suggest that if you really have your heart set on a split breast, you cut it yourself. You'll find it's easy and quick, and you'll pay less in the long run. Here's how to cut a breast into split breast halves:

1. Pull the skin across the whole breast so that it covers the meat evenly. Place the breast on the cutting board, skin-side down.

2. Align your thumb and the edge of your palm along the rib cage and push the rib cage out and down toward the surface of the cutting board. This will crack the seam between the rib cage and the keel bone. (The keel bone is dark on top, turning into softer white cartilage as it comes to a point at the bottom of the breast.)

3. Use the point of a boning knife to trace around the keel bone. Grab the top of the bone and pull it out cleanly.

Chicken tenders: The chicken tender is the juiciest, most tender, and most flavorful part of the breast. The filet mignon of the chicken, it runs under the bottom of the breast meat, next to the bone, and is sold at a higher price. If you are shopping for chicken tenders, rather than a boneless chicken breast, beware. Because of that higher price, boneless breast meat is sometimes cut down and sold as tenders. You can tell a true chicken tender because it will have a white sinew running along the top, and it will be flat and shiny on one side and rough and dull on the other.

What to look for: When shopping for chicken breast, you want to make sure the skin (if it isn't skinless) is well dimpled and shiny. The meat should be pinkish if it's grade A (see page 021) or light brown if it's free-range or organic (see page 017). Milky white lines in the meat are evidence that it is going bad. If the breast was split, check the bone end at the joint where the wing was removed; it should be whitish gray and shiny.

How to cook it: Whatever chicken breast cut you prefer, the skin and bone will help protect the meat during cooking. You can roast a whole breast in the oven at 375°F [190°C] for 35 to 45 minutes. I personally find that grilling chicken breasts is the best way to cook them. If you want to grill chicken breast, I suggest you buy whole boneless breasts, still connected in the middle. Marinate them overnight, and then open them up flat when you put them on the grill. Cook them over a medium fire for 12 to 15 minutes per side and let them rest for 10 minutes before cutting them neatly in half.

For skin-on, bone-in breasts, grill them skin-side up in an aluminum pan for 30 to 35 minutes. In any case, you should always let grilled chicken rest for 10 minutes after cooking.

Cutlets

Cutlets are just thin slices of breast meat. Many people like them because they seem like they would be easy to cook, and for their low fat content and portion size. But with no skin it's hard to keep cutlets from drying out. For that reason, they should be at least 1/8 in [4 mm] thick, so that there is enough meat to plump during cooking and the cut will retain some moisture.

What to look for: Look for packaged cutlets that are all the same color and the same thickness, so that one end of a cutlet is not thicker than the other.

How to cook it: Breading and panfrying cutlets helps keep them moist and allows you to add flavor in the spices of the breading. Serve them with a little marinara or provolone melted on top, and you've made the most out of a very modest poultry cut.

Wings

The simplest of foods can provide a great culinary experience. That's why I love chicken wings. There should be a picture of wings right next to "finger food" in the dictionary, because your hands are the best utensils for eating them. The wing has two joints: the **drumette** (the part closest to the body) and the wing itself.

What to look for: The wing proper is sweeter and more tender than the drumette. You can find these in stores, labeled "wing flings." Drumettes are more popular because they have more meat, but that popularity translates to higher cost. I like the flings for their more consistent quality, better flavor, and superior tenderness. Whenever you're picking out wings, avoid any that are bruised or have blood spots. Feel the package to ensure that there are no broken bones.

How to cook it: Fry or bake wings until almost done, and then coat them in your favorite barbecue sauce and finish them off on the grill. This will leave them flavorful, with a crispy skin.

037

PORK

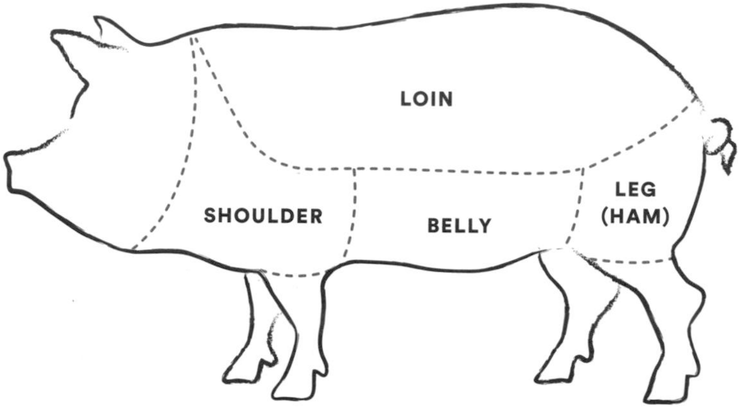

LOIN

SHOULDER

BELLY

LEG (HAM)

If I had a nickel for every time a customer told me that she wanted her family (or, more specifically, her husband) to eat more healthfully, but she just couldn't stand the thought of serving yet another skinless chicken breast, well, I'd be one very rich butcher. Every time I had that conversation, I directed my customer right to pork.

    The most wonderful thing about "the other white meat" is diversity. Yes, most pork cuts are leaner and more healthful than their beef equivalents and right on a par with any chicken cut. A pork tenderloin contains a lot more flavor than a chicken breast or tenders, with no more fat. Pork is also versatile and easy to cook. Of course, if you're looking for some over-the-top flavor and you don't mind a little more fat with your dinner, you can turn to delectable ribs or pork belly. Really, the pig has it all.

And there has never been a better time to buy and cook pork. The cuts have never been leaner, and the danger of getting sick from trichinosis has been eliminated thanks to USDA feeding and husbandry regulations. That's why the USDA lowered the recommended doneness temperature for pork from 185°F [85°C] to 160°F [71°C]. The bonus? Now you can cook the pork you buy to a nice pink blush and wind up with a very juicy, tender piece of meat.

Shopping for pork is just as easy, because pigs are simpler animals than steers and just about every single cut that comes off a pig is widely available. The only real choice you'll face (well, other than which delicious cut entices you the most) is whether to buy meat from industrial or naturally raised animals. The flavor differences between an industrial-raised animal and its pastured brother are noticeable. That's because more than any other animal, a pig's diet is reflected in the flavor of the meat. Industrial pigs are fed a bland, fattening diet, usually heavy on the corn syrup and corn processing by-products, and light on anything intensely flavorful. Pigs raised in pastures follow their nature. They are rooters who will eat tubers, fungi (until very recently, pigs were used to hunt truffles in France and Italy), and even forest debris such as acorns. A wild or close-to-wild diet will give the pork a rich, distinctive flavor.

039

Unfortunately, it requires more time and effort to raise a pastured pig, so depending on where you live, it may be difficult to find anything but industrial pork. Regardless, you will still enjoy a satisfying flavor and healthful meat.

Most of the pork in U.S. stores today is either American or Canadian. The Canadian pork is leaner but not quite as flavorful. It has become popular because it is not only leaner, but it is also less expensive than what producers in the United States offer.

Ray's ADVICE

Avoid cross-contamination. The USDA recommends—and I heartily second—cleaning surfaces, including cutting boards, knives, and your hands, thoroughly after handling each type of meat. I make that easy by using different color-coded cutting boards in my kitchen—red for pork, natural wood for beef, and green for chicken. That way I never risk cross-contamination when I'm in a rush and preparing a large meal.

Regardless of the type of pork you're buying, picking a fresh package is key. It's common industry practice to rewrap packaged pork, so you need to look carefully at what's inside. Any bones should be white and bright, not dull or gray. The meat should be pinkish white (Canadian) or tannish white (American). All packaged pork should have a wet sheen. Avoid cuts with flecks of red through the meat—these indicate that the animal was stressed prior to slaughter. You should also stay away from cuts where the bone is darkened or there is a lot of blood or moisture in the package. That package has been around too long to be considered fresh, and the meat will likely wind up dry and tasteless.

There are four pork primals, from front to back: **shoulder, loin, belly,** and **leg (ham).**

Ground Pork (not pictured)
Ground pork is usually fattier than any other pork product, and more so than ground turkey or chicken. This is actually desirable because pork fat is a versatile cooking ingredient. Not only is it incredibly flavorful, but the fat is also softer and melts in a more uniform and predictable manner than other animal fats. That's why ground pork is most often used as an additional element, rather than a principal ingredient. You can easily grind your own pork from high-quality shoulder meat with regular marbling (the

040

Ray's ADVICE

A leaner meat, such as pork, is much more sensitive to the freezing process than a fattier protein. Pork also has a lot of water in it, but it loses moisture quickly after it is cut. That's why I freeze it immediately if I'm not cooking it the same day I buy it. Fortunately, pork's alluring, rich flavor holds up very well to freezing. Follow these guidelines when freezing your pork purchases.

Wrap pork correctly to avoid damage in the freezer. Use freezer paper (waxed side facing the meat), heavy-duty aluminum foil, heavy-duty plastic wrap, or a thick, resealable freezer bag. Be careful with bone ends and wrap them securely so that they don't puncture the freezer wrapping. Wrap the meat as tightly as possible, eliminating as much air as you can from inside the package. Last, always label the package with the cut and date it went into the freezer.

Cook pork immediately after it has thawed. According to the USDA, pork thawed in the refrigerator can be refrozen, but this is generally not a good practice. Refreezing thawed meat of any kind dehydrates the meat and makes it tougher when cooked. In any case, never, ever refreeze meat that has been thawed to room temperature. Bacterial and microbial action has been started that will continue, even if the pork is refrozen.

041

amount of fat veining running throughout the meat)—it's inexpensive, widely available, and delicious. However, most people find it more convenient just to pick up a package of ground pork.

What to look for: It's easy to tell the relative fat content of ground pork by looking at the package. A light, almost tan color is best, and there should be absolutely no liquid visible in the package. The lighter the meat in the package, the more fat it contains. In any case, the strands of meat should always look soft and moist.

How to cook it: Like any good Italian, I use a mixture of meats, including ground pork, in my meatballs, meat loaf, and *sugo di carne* (Italian meat sauce). The pork fat is unrivaled for maintaining moisture in something like a meatball, and it adds a light but rich flavor as well. Like all ground meat, ground pork must be cooked to 160°F [71°C], rather than the 145°F [63°C] recommended for other pork cuts.

SHOULDER

The shoulder is a hard-working area on a squat animal like a pig. The whole shoulder is large, and it is usually broken down into a **roast** (the bottom portion) and what's known as a **butt** (the top). Shoulder meat offers some wonderful flavor, but it's also full of connective tissue, which has to be broken down. That's why the shoulder cuts are the pork of choice among barbecuers willing to tend the grill for true low-and-slow barbecuing—long cooking times are best for breaking down connective tissue. Pork shoulder makes for incredible pulled pork. Expect any roast cut from the shoulder to feed six to eight people.

009

Picnic Roast (also known as Pork Picnic Shoulder or Cali)

This is a crude cut from the butcher's perspective; it takes little skill to remove because it is cut with most of the foreshank (front shin bone) in the roast. The meat in the picnic roast is coarse textured and hearty, and the flavor is slightly richer and stronger than butt cuts.

042

What to look for: Once you decide that you want to cook a picnic roast, you're about done. The cut is one of the first a butcher makes in breaking down a pig, and if you're not buying from a butcher, chances are the whole roast was simply shrink-wrapped in Cryo-vac packaging and shipped to the store. Check the expiration date; you'll want to be as far ahead of that date as possible. You won't see much meat through the fat cap when looking at the cut, but you should make sure that the fat is bright white and the skin on the bottom is unbroken and uncut—the sign of a properly butchered picnic roast. When buying a picnic roast in Cryovac packaging, a little blood is to be expected, but it should be light red and clear. Darker red or cloudy blood is a sign that the meat is starting to turn. No blood whatsoever in the package can be an indication that the cut was deep frozen, which can result in a weaker flavor.

How to cook it: You can make absolutely delicious barbecued pulled pork by roasting a picnic roast nice and slow, instead of barbecuing it, which is a much more involved process. Start the roast off in a 425°F [220°C] oven for about 45 minutes, and then lower the temperature to 225°F [110°C] and let it cook for 8 to 9 hours more. You want an internal temperature of 160°F [71°C]. After removing it from the oven, let it rest for about 15 minutes before shredding. I like to shred the pork with my hands, rather than a fork. The meat retains more moisture that way. If the roast is too hot to handle, it hasn't rested enough. Many cooks pull off the skin first and crisp it by cutting it into pieces and putting it in a 400°F [200°C] oven for 10 to 15 minutes. You can even buy pork skin already cooked this way; it is known as pork crackling.

Shoulder Butt (also known as Boston Butt)

This cut is taken from higher on the animal than the picnic roast, right above the shoulder blade. Even though the name includes the words "shoulder" and "butt," it is actually the pig's neck. The cut has less connective tissue and is much meatier, with better marbling than the picnic roast. In fact, it's the most marbled cut in the entire animal, making it the cut of choice for pork sausage. The extra fat also means the cut can be cooked more quickly than the picnic roast and still have a wonderful texture and rich pork flavor. It also lacks the large piece of leg bone of the picnic roast, which makes it more attractive to many home cooks.

What to look for: I prefer to buy a shoulder butt that weighs around 6 lb [2.7 kg]. You can find much larger ones, but the smaller cuts are more flavorful. The shoulder butt should be fairly lean, with a solid white cover of fat along the bottom.

How to cook it: The best way to cook shoulder butt is to treat it as the roast that it is. Coat it with your favorite lightly seasoned rub, set it on a rack in a roasting pan, and add a small amount of liquid—2 cups [480 ml] of vegetable broth works fine. The roast will need only about 3 hours in a 350°F [180°C] oven, after which it will slice like butter.

Pork Neck Bones

011

Let's be clear here, these are called "bones" because you can't expect a lot of meat on them. But because the neck is the most marbled area of the pig, the meat that surrounds the neck bones tastes a lot like the best pork sausage. That great flavor is why neck bones are used for many different styles of cooking and are a classic soul-food ingredient.

What to look for: Chances are you're only going to find neck bones at a butcher shop or a high-end market with a butcher on staff. (These bones are so good for flavoring cooking that I made sure they were available in every meat department I ever ran.) The meat is a little darker than the shoulder butt, but should be nicely marbled, with a moist sheen. The only bone you should see is along the bottom, and it should be slightly off-white to very light gray.

How to cook it: Time is the secret ingredient for cooking pork neck bones. They are commonly smoked (and often sold that way) but are even more often used as a base for Southern dishes like neck bones and gravy. For that dish, about 2 lb [910 kg] of neck bones are slow-roasted for hours in 4 cups [960 ml] or more of chicken broth. I prefer to throw mine in a slow cooker with a combination of root vegetables and about 3 cups [720 ml] of chicken stock. Let it cook all day, and the meat will fall off the bone.

044

LOIN

This is the leanest and most tender area of the animal, yielding melt-in-your-mouth roasts and chops (that is, if you cook them correctly). Loins are sometimes roasted whole, but more often this section is broken down into individual cuts. The nature of the cut depends on where in the loin it comes from. **Blade** or **rib end cuts** are taken close to the shoulder and come with a good amount of fat, while cuts from the other end, the loin or **sirloin** end, are leaner. The **center cuts** are the leanest part of the loin, and are premium.

Rib End Roast

This roast is sold bone-in and boneless. It is the least expensive of all pork roasts, because it has a good deal of connective tissue and tougher meat. A little careful cooking is all you need to exploit its wonderful pork flavor.

What to look for: The meat on the rib end roast may be two-toned, but that is totally normal. If you decide to buy it with the bone in, ask the butcher to crack, or cut through, the chine bone (back bone) to make the roast easier to slice. I prefer a boneless rib end roast because the blade bone (shoulder blade) in the rib end does not add flavor and is extremely hard to carve around once cooked. Buy boneless, and you get more of what you are paying for. The abundant marbling of this cut makes it one of the most flavorful even without the bone.

How to cook it: Slow-cook this cut with 4 to 6 cups [960 ml to 1.4 L] of liquid. I cook it in a Dutch oven over low heat with 4 cups [960 ml] water, 1 cup [240 ml] cranberry juice, one 15-oz [430-g] can jellied cranberry sauce, and 1/2 cup [100 g] sugar. Cook it on low for 2 hours per 1 lb [455 g].

045

Rib Blade Chops (also known as Rib End Chops)

013

These chops are taken from the shoulder end of the loin, right behind the shoulder butt. Don't make the mistake of confusing these with pork blade steak, a fattier shoulder cut. These chops are leaner than pork blade steak, but have more fat than the adjacent center-cut chop.

What to look for: Like most other pork chops, these are sold bone-in, which aids in cooking. Look for a thick cut (or order thick-cut chops from your butcher). I prefer a blade chop at least 1 in [2.5 cm] thick. The meat should be light to dark tan, with soft white fat. It is not unusual for the chop to be two-toned, with light and dark meat.

How to cook it: These are the perfect pork chops for braising in a slightly acidic liquid, which will help break down the connective tissue and tougher portions of the meat. I braise my blade chops in apple cider with red wine vinegar; the flavor mix is as close to perfect as you'll see in this world.

Country-Style Spareribs

014

Country-style spareribs are meaty and full of flavor, though they are not actually ribs. They are made by cutting the rib end into 1½- to 2-in- [4- to 5-cm-] thick pieces. They are then cut again through the middle, creating two pieces that look like ribs, with a section of the blade bone in one half and the back rib bone in the other. (So, strictly speaking, they are not actually ribs.) Country-style spare-ribs are one of the most affordable cuts in the meat case.

What to look for: Country-style spareribs cut from the loin end (closest the back of the animal) are not as good as those from the rib end. Look for more marbling and lighter-colored meat, which indicates the "ribs" came from the rib end.

How to cook it: Start by placing the spareribs in an acidic marinade to help tenderize the meat. Then do what I do, put the spareribs in a slow cooker with your favorite barbecue sauce at 250°F [120°C] for 4 to 6 hours. Remove them from the slow cooker and put them on a wooden barbecue plank (to contain the mess and keep the ribs from sticking), brush with more barbecue sauce, and grill over medium-high heat for 10 to 15 minutes, just until they get a nice crust on the outside.

Pork Loin Roast (also known as Center Loin Roast)

This is a favorite roast of home cooks because it delivers flavor fireworks with very little fuss in the kitchen. It can feed anywhere from four to ten people, with a salad and couple of side dishes. Leftovers keep for up to 1 week and make wonderful sandwiches. Bone-in loin roasts benefit greatly from the bone, which adds quite a bit of flavor and keeps the meat moist under high-heat cooking. The downside is that the bone (a piece of the backbone in this case) makes the cooked roast a little difficult to slice into manageable portions. That's why many people opt for a boneless pork loin roast, which also gives the cook the option of stuffing it.

What to look for: You'll be well served by a loin roast that weighs in around 6 lb [2.7 kg]. I buy a bone-in roast and have the bone cracked (ask the butcher to "crack the chine"), to make slicing the meat easier. The bone adds so much flavor that I think the difference is noticeable.

How to cook it: Roasting is the only way I would ever cook this terrific piece of pork. Many cooks like to smear it with a rub before cooking it in dry heat. I prefer to season it with salt and pepper, sear the roast first on all sides for 2 to 3 minutes per side, and then roast it in a 400°F [200°C] oven for about 25 minutes. The flavor and juiciness will knock your socks off. If you would rather not deal with a bone but want to keep the roast moist, here is a little trick: Have the butcher cut a boneless roast into two equal pieces. Place one piece on top of the other, meat against meat, with the fat on the outside. Tie the pieces together to form one thicker roast with a fat cover all the way around to protect the roast. As they cook, the two pieces will adhere together and, when they're done, they will slice like a single roast.

047

Pork Crown Roast

016

This is by far my favorite holiday roast. It's easy to cook, feeds a big crowd, and makes for a festive presentation on the table. I even prefer this over lamb crown roast because it has great flavor and costs less. The roast is formed of two bone-in, center-cut pork loins. The rib bones are Frenched (see page 011) and the chine bone, or backbone, is cracked, pulled into a circle, and tied in place to create the appearance of a crown. Not only is it a unique look, the bones on the outside protect the meat from drying out, making this one of the juiciest roasts you'll ever taste. Stuffing can stretch the meal even further, allowing you feed a crowd with less meat.

What to look for: You generally choose a crown roast based more on the number of chops in the roast, rather than on its weight. Consider what you're serving with the roast and determine how many chops each person will eat. For example, if you decide 1½ chops per person is about right and you're going to serve eight people, you'll order a 12-chop crown roast. The roast can actually be made as big as 24 chops. You want to make sure that the two sections used to form the crown are identical in size, and that the chine bone has been cracked by the butcher. A crown roast can be made of just one center-cut pork loin, but I don't suggest buying it that way. The meat ends up tearing open between the bones when pulled into a circle, and it will dry out when cooked. For the same reason, a crown roast should be no smaller than 12 chops (6 chops on each side). The bones in any crown roast should be white to light gray, and don't be afraid of the fat. The inside of the crown, where the meat is showing, should have a light fat cover, which should be soft and white.

How to cook it: Wrap aluminum foil around the exposed rib bones to keep them from blackening during cooking. Start roasting the crown at 500°F [260°C] for the first 15 minutes, then lower the temperature to 375°F [190°C] for the remaining time—about 15 minutes more per 1 lb [455 g]. You want an internal meat temperature of 145°F [63°C]. Let the roast rest for 12 to 15 minutes,

048

then remove the foil on the bones, slice, and serve. It's best to cook any stuffing separately to avoid possible cross-contamination. Place it in the center of the roast right before serving.

Center-Cut Pork Chops

017

Although the center of the pork loin is lean, it is full of flavor, which is why it's so popular. These chops start at the beginning of the rib section and run to the beginning of the sirloin, which means they come in slightly different sizes and shapes.

What to look for: Whether you're buying center-cut chops from a butcher or out of the case, you'll want to be absolutely sure that they really are center-cut chops. Chops from the rib side will be round, with what is known as a deckle of marbled meat running along the top ¼ in [6 mm] of the chop. If the deckle is thicker than that, it isn't a true center-cut chop. The best center-cut chops come from the loin end and contain a classic T-shaped bone, which makes the chops look like small T-bone steaks. The bone, if there is one, should be the same thickness on both sides of the chop, and the tenderloin on the bottom of the bone should be rounder, leaner, and darker than the meat at the top of the bone. Keep in mind that these chops are cut from a relatively lean area of the animal. That means that thickness matters. Only buy chops at least 1 in [2.5 cm] thick, and cut evenly across. Because keeping such a lean cut moist during cooking is crucial, I buy only bone-in center-cut chops. The underside of the bone should be lined with a white opaque membrane. If it's transparent, and you can see the bone through it, the chop is too old and has lost its moisture. The meat itself should be white to beige if it's American pork, and white to light pink if it is Canadian.

049

How to cook it: I know many people love to bread and fry pork chops, but that doesn't do a quality cut like these justice. I season them as I would a steak—a little kosher salt and freshly ground pepper, a coating of olive oil, and maybe a sprinkling of chopped rosemary—and then sear them in a pan over high heat, 4 to 5 minutes

per side. You want the interior temperature to be around 140°F [60°C]. Leave them to rest for 5 minutes; they will continue to cook (known as carry-over cooking) to medium-rare and will reach the requisite 145°F [63°C].

Tenderloin

018

050

This is the most tender cut in a pig, and one of my favorite cuts among all meats. Pork tenderloin is the perfect combination of lean, tender, flavorful, and easy to cook. The flavor holds up well to freezing and the meat thaws quickly, making it a great item to stock up on whenever it's on sale. Pork tenderloin is often sold in two pieces in a heavy Cryovac bag, which can go directly into the freezer. The cut is long and boneless, making it easy to slice into individual portions. There are many ways to cook this naturally luscious treat, but only one way to go wrong: overcooking. Dry out pork tenderloin, and you've done it an injustice.

What to look for: If you prefer not to do a lot of prep to your meat, buy a cut with the silverskin, or membrane, already removed. If it's attached, you will need to remove it before you cook (see page 123). You'll sometimes find tenderloin presliced. I'd avoid that because such lean, tender meat can dry out very quickly when sliced, and it shrinks more when cooked than a bigger piece. Even if you're not going to use all the tenderloin, I'd strongly urge you to buy one whole, cut off what you need, and freeze the rest. The tenderloin is extremely lean with no marbling and a dark pink-purple color. The lighter the color, the sweeter the tenderloin will be. Beware of a store-wrapped pork tenderloin; Cryovac wrapping is so common that store wrapping often indicates that an older tenderloin has been repackaged.

How to cook it: One of the easiest and best ways to cook this cut is by roasting it under high heat. I use an herb blend in olive oil as a rub, and then I cook the tenderloin in a 450°F [230°C] oven. I cook it about 12 minutes, flip it, and let it cook for another 10 to 12 minutes. Let it rest for 10 minutes (the internal temperature will be 160°F [71°C]) and, bam, you've got yourself a flavorful, juicy, fork-tender piece of meat.

Sirloin Roast (also known as Loin End Roast)

019

This roast is taken from the sirloin end of the pork loin, just in front of the leg, and is richly flavored and very tender. You can buy the roast boneless or bone-in. Either way, the cut is good value for your money and a leaner alternative to beef roasts.

What to look for: Home cooks sometimes have trouble carving this roast with the bone in, because it contains parts of the hip bone and the backbone. Unless you're good with a knife, I suggest you have a butcher bone and tie the roast—it will be much easier to handle.

How to cook it: Because this cut is relatively lean, it's best cooked with a traditional dry-roasting method. Coat the roast with your favorite dry rub and then place it in a roasting pan on a rack. I add 1 in [2.5 cm] of liquid to the bottom of the pan, half white wine and half water, to keep the meat moist. Cook an average-size sirloin roast at 375°F [190°C] for about 1 hour. The internal temperature should be about 145°F [63°C] when you take it out of the oven. Let it rest for 10 minutes, and it will be ready to serve.

051

020

Pork Sirloin Chops (also known as Loin End Chops)

The sirloin end from where these chops are taken is full of flavor, and these are the leanest of all the chop cuts. These are delicious but require careful preparation and cooking to keep them from becoming tough and flavorless.

What to look for: The meat on these lean chops will be dark, and they will have more bone than other pork chops. The bone is also bigger on one side than it is on the other. Keep that in mind when looking at packaged chops, because the bone you see will most likely be the smaller side. Try to buy chops that are ½ to ¾ in [12 mm to 2 cm] thick—you'll only need one chop per person.

How to cook it: I pan-sear the chops in a large saucepan, giving them a nice crust. Then I finish them in the same pan full of vegetables with 2 to 3 cups [480 to 720 ml] of vegetable broth (or, for a bit more unique flavor, beer). The chops wind up very tender, and it's an easy, one-pan meal for a fast and filling weeknight dinner.

021

Pork Cutlets

This is my favorite cutlet. The flavor and juiciness of pork holds up remarkably well to breading and frying. Although pork cutlets come from the most-tender part of the animal, they are thin, and they need to be cooked carefully to keep them from drying out. That said, they are also incredibly adaptable—it's easy to find dozens of great recipes for pork cutlets.

What to look for: The best cutlets come from the sirloin (loin end) of the pork loin. People often make the mistake of spending top dollar for center-cut pork cutlets, only to have them wind up dry and tasteless. The sirloin has a stronger flavor and stays tender even when sliced thin. Thin is relative; buy cutlets ⅛ to ¼ in [4 to 6 mm] thick. The cutlets in each package should be the same size and thickness.

How to cook it: Many cooks bread and fry pork cutlets, which is a natural way to prepare them. Add your favorite spices to the breading mix, and it's fairly simple to get dinner on the table. However, I prefer to cook cutlets in a heavy, flavorful sauce (marsala is my favorite). The cutlet becomes a stage for the flavors in the sauce, and cooking the cutlets in the same pan ensures they will be tender and moist when you serve them.

Baby Back Ribs

022

This is the section of ribs between the spine and spareribs, and is where the rib bones start. They are the bones you find on the back of a center-cut pork loin. They are called "baby" because the bones are thinner and shorter than other ribs. That said, they are incredibly meaty and delectable. A rack of baby back ribs will be wider on one end than on the other, often about 6 in [15 cm] on end side and 3 in [7.5 cm], on the other.

What to look for: True baby back rib racks weigh less than 1¾ lb [800 g]. Because they are such a treat, I always buy my baby back ribs from a butcher. Supermarkets usually stock mass-produced boxes that arrive partially frozen and have much less flavor. These are also one of the most commonly prepackaged and branded meat items. Unfortunately, prepackaged baby backs are often enhanced with preservative fluid that adds saltiness. I much prefer the unadulterated flavor of fresh baby back ribs, and I think most people who have tasted both would agree.

Ray's ADVICE

053

Many pork cuts are classic barbecue offerings. But no matter what you're grilling or barbecuing, never start by dousing the meat in barbecue sauce. Despite the name, the sauce is ideally used as a condiment. If you're going to put it on during cooking, do it right at the end. Otherwise, the sugars in the sauce will burn and give the meat an unpleasant charred taste.

How to cook it: Baby backs have less fat and more flavor than other pork rib cuts, which means they will cook more quickly. Even so, you can smoke, barbecue, or grill these beauties. Use a rub and keep an eye on the ribs so that you don't overcook them. It's also wise to add a drip pan in the grill, right under the ribs. Fill it with beer or water to regulate the temperature and make sure the meat is kept moist, tender, and flavorful.

Spareribs

023 Spareribs are the stock-in-trade of barbecue road joints, from Memphis to Kansas City. Real spareribs are cut from the shoulder to the end of the rib cage on the pig. Spareribs come in sizes that reflect the age of the animal. The most common is a 4- to 7-lb [1.8- to 3.2-kg] rack of ribs, but smaller racks are better.

What to look for: Barbecuers, aficionados, and butchers like me all prefer the spareribs known as "3½ down," meaning the weight is less than 3½ lb [1.6 kg]. The meat on these smaller ribs is lighter, sweeter, and more tender. You can buy them in slabs, but they are also regularly cut down into more manageable portions. Regardless of size or portion, the meat should completely cover the bone. (Inexperienced butchers sometimes cut too close to the bone, creating what those in the business call a "shiner," a sign of poor preparation.) The meat should have a moist sheen and be very light tan, with marbling running through it.

054

Buy the freshest spareribs you can find, and never buy ribs that have been frozen. You'll know because the meat will be discolored, the edges will look dehydrated, and the ends of the bones will be black. You might find ribs in plastic Cryovac packages, but that doesn't necessarily mean they were frozen; look for the words "previously frozen" on the package. Reject any package if there is a significant amount of liquid inside. Be sure that 3½ down spareribs are actually that, and not larger ribs that have been cut down. Very wide rib bones are signs that the ribs have come from an older, larger animal and have been cut down.

St. Louis–cut ribs are a rack that has had the sternum, cartilage, and rib tips removed to make the rack easier to handle. The trimmed rack is perfectly rectangular and ideal for cooking on a grill. The cut is preferred by many true barbecuers and by home cooks who don't want to deal with trimming up the rack themselves. St. Louis ribs are usually offered wherever spareribs are sold, and any butcher will trim a rack for you.

How to cook it: The best way to cook spareribs is low-and-slow barbecuing. Cook them at a steady 255° to 260°F [124° to 127°C] for at least 4 hours over indirect heat. Ribs are usually treated with a wet or dry rub (use your favorite recipe from the bazillions available in cookbooks or on the Internet) and cooked with wood smoke. The wood can be the primary fuel source, or you can use a foil pouch of fruitwood chips placed on gas burners or on coals.

BELLY

You know you're in a true, old-time, high-quality butcher shop when they have fresh-cut pork belly on offer. There is so much you can do with this. It can be smoked for the ultimate homemade bacon or used in a wide variety of dishes for its exceptional flavor.

055

024

Pork Belly (Whole)

Pork belly is an incredibly versatile boneless cut, with layers of fat and rich, flavorful meat used in Asian and Chinese cooking. Americans are usually most familiar with one product of cured pork belly—bacon. But there is far more to this cut than bacon. It can be diced and stir-fried, cooked sous vide, roasted, and barbecued.

What to look for: In addition to old-fashioned butcher shops, you'll find fresh pork belly in some gourmet shops and ethnic food stores. But it might be easier to find online. The cut should have a thick layer of skin, tan to light brown. Layers of white fat should be interspersed with strands of pink to reddish meat. Although the cut is mostly fat, always look for a piece that is as lean—meaty—as possible.

How to cook it: I prefer my pork belly with a crispy skin, and I like to cook it in apple cider or wine to complement—and cut—the natural richness of the meat. Begin by rubbing the skin of the pork belly lightly with a little white vinegar. Sprinkle a little salt over the skin to help crisp it and then place it skin-side up in a roasting pan. Roast the belly at 240°F [115°C] for 30 minutes, or until the skin starts to crackle. Then add enough wine or cider to reach halfway up the sides of the pan. Lower the heat to 170°F [75°C] and cook for another 1½ hours, adding more liquid as needed. Let the belly rest for 15 minutes after cooking and then slice it skin-side down.

025 (a)

Salt Pork

Salt pork is nothing more than pork belly that has been salted and cured, without being smoked. The skin has been removed.

What to look for: Salt pork is easier to come by than fresh pork belly, and you'll likely find a prepackaged slab at your local super-market. Do not, however, confuse salt pork with fatback. Although they look similar, fatback is not from the belly; it's from the fat that runs along the back. They are easy to tell apart because fatback has no meat running through it.

How to cook it: Salt pork can be used to add intense flavor and moisture to dishes as varied as white beans and salt pork, or Brussels sprouts with salt pork.

056

Bacon

Bacon is cut from cured and smoked pork bellies. Slab bacon is exactly as it sounds—unsliced bacon. Buying slab bacon allows you to cut it to your desired thickness or cube it for cooking purposes. Sliced or slab, bacon is a raw product that must be cooked before it's consumed. Different woods and flavorings are used in the curing process to vary the taste, for example apple wood–smoked or maple-flavored bacon.

What to look for: The bigger the piece of meat, the better it will retain flavor and moisture. That's why buying slab bacon can be a smart strategy if your family eats a good amount of bacon. Slab bacon is less expensive and has fewer additives than packaged sliced bacon, but you'll need to buy it from a butcher. Look for medium- to dark-brown skin on the bottom. The fat on the outside should be light yellow, and you should see streaks of meat running through it. When you're shopping for that perfect package of bacon, turn it over. Just because the bacon looks lean through the front window doesn't mean you're seeing the whole picture. The higher the ratio of meat to fat, the better. Although bacon has one of the longest shelf lives of packaged meat, it will still lose flavor over time. Ideally, look for a package with at least 15 days to go before the use-by date.

How to cook it: Bacon is simple to cook, but controlling the splatter is key. I lay the strips in a hot nonstick pan and cover it with aluminum foil while it cooks. Flip the strips once and cook them as crispy as you like. Of course, bacon is also terrific in other recipes. I wrap beef fillet with strips to keep it moist and add a little smoky flavor. You can also cube slab bacon and use it in a stew or soup.

057

THE MANY FACES OF BACON

Other countries have their own unique ways of making bacon, and all are delicious. The common factor in all of these is that the bacon is cured with a combination of salt and spices.

Italy: Pancetta

Although similar to American bacon, pancetta is not smoked. It is sold in two forms: rolled and sliced thin. Sliced pancetta is generally eaten cold, as part of an antipasto platter. Rolled pancetta is often cubed or sliced and used in cooking in much the same way American bacon is. Rolled pancetta is actually a nice substitute for American bacon in dishes where a smoky flavor would not be appropriate.

United Kingdom: Irish Bacon (also known as Irish Back Bacon)

In the British Isles, this is known simply as "bacon," but an American would detect the difference. The bacon is cured but not smoked, and it is made from the loin, rather than the belly. Like American bacon, it must be cooked before eating, but it is much leaner and meatier than its New World cousin. The hearty centerpiece of a traditional English breakfast, it makes an interesting change from the American version, although you'll have to look hard to find it. Irish bacon is considered a specialty meat item.

Canada: Canadian Bacon

Lean meat from the loin is cured and then hot-smoked to create this component of eggs Benedict; it's also a common pizza topping. The product is fully cooked when packaged and has a milder, leaner flavor that tastes more like ham than the smoky flavor associated with American bacon.

058

LEG (HAM)

The leg is a large primal with the thickest fat cover of any cut over the most flavorful parts of the animal. The amount of fat cover and meat make leg cuts, such as ham, ideal for roasting or smoking. The ham is actually the most popular cut on the leg, but the ham comes in many forms—there's a ham for any occasion and preference. The bones themselves should not be ignored; the flavor-rich marrow and the nature of the meat that clings to the lower leg, make leg bones fantastic flavoring agents in a wide range of dishes. Although they are an acquired taste, even the feet find their way to the plate.

Leg (also known as Fresh Ham)

026

The fresh ham is the biggest and leanest of pork roasts. Despite its name, once a fresh ham is cooked, it will be white and tasty and will eat like pork chops. It has skin around three-quarters of the cut and a nice fat layer, making this cut ideal for roasting in dry, high-temperature heat.

What to look for: If you are feeding a large crowd, a boned leg, rolled and tied, can be a great option, but you'll need a butcher to prepare it for you. Because the cut is large—14 to 20 lb [6.3 to 9 kg]— the leg is often cut down and sold as either a shank half ham or a butt half ham. The shank half makes a better presentation and is easier to carve. The butt half is more tender and has a bit more flavor, but is harder to carve because of the hip bone.

How to cook it: The thick layer of fat on a fresh ham is so flavorful that the only seasoning you need is a little salt and pepper. There is nothing like the taste of the crispy skin on a roasted fresh ham. Roast the ham in a 325°F [165°C] oven until the ham's internal temperature reaches 160°F [71°C] for medium—roughly 20 minutes per 1 lb [455 g]. Let the ham rest for 10 to 15 minutes, slice, and serve. One caveat, though, the crisp skin on a roasted fresh ham is not only difficult to slice through, it can even dull the sharpest of knives. Remove the skin before slicing the meat, chop the skin into pieces, and add it to the platter before serving.

059

Smoked Ham

027

Smoked ham is some of the most delicious—and most popular—meat on a pig. The hams are sold fully cooked and can be served hot or cold. They are sold dry or wet cured. Dry-cured hams are much saltier because they are cured with salty rubs. They are called country or Virginia hams because they are most common in the South. The cuts are the same as for fresh hams. You'll find whole bone-in smoked hams as well as smoked shank half hams and smoked butt half hams.

What to look for: I always buy bone-in hams because boneless hams are pressed into a uniform shape after the bone is removed, which can translate to a lot more processing and lost flavor, not to mention a weird texture. Depending on whether you buy a whole ham, shank half, or butt half, the bone can make carving a challenge. That's why the most popular smoked ham, and one that has become a holiday staple, is the spiral-sliced ham. Spiral hams are precut by machine into thin slices down to the bone, so that you can have a beautiful presentation on the table and easily remove the slices. All you need to do is heat the ham, and it's ready to serve. Plan on feeding two people for every 1 lb [455 g] of bone-in ham. Because boneless hams are very lean with no waste, you should figure 4 oz [115 g] per person. Keep in mind that ham makes spectacular leftovers—I always buy extra. The meat will keep for at least 2 weeks refrigerated.

060

How to cook it: A smoked ham is ready to eat, although most people prefer to serve it hot. Warm up a precooked ham, following the instructions on the packaging, to an internal temperature of 140°F [60°C] and let it rest for 10 minutes. The only downside to a spiral ham is that the slices are thin and can dry out during heating. That's why I always recommend using a glaze with a spiral ham. It ensures the meat will remain moist, and is a great way to add a personal touch and flavor to your ham.

A big issue you'll face when shopping for any ham other than a country ham is water content. Wet curing involves moisture, and the more moisture that is added, the more it will dilute the natural flavor of the meat. A ham labeled simply "ham" has the least amount of added fluid. The more diluted products are—in order of saturation—"ham with natural juices," "ham, water added," and "ham and water product." The best-tasting ham in the meat case is generally the one with the lowest water content.

Ham Steak (not pictured)

Like the ham itself, ham steaks are sold bone-in and boneless. Either way, this is a fantastic cut that doesn't get the attention it deserves. A ham steak is cut from the center of the ham and is a versatile piece of meat.

What to look for: A traditional ham steak comes with the bone, and that's the way I buy it. The bone identifies the steak as an actual cut from the leg and not a piece of pressed and formed ham. Look for steaks close to 1 in [2.5 cm] thick, with a narrow band of white fat along one side, and a uniform pink color throughout. The bone should be round and slightly off-center.

How to cook it: Although some people grill or broil it, I think the only legitimate way to cook this cut is to pan-sear it. Cook the steak over medium-high heat for about 5 minutes per side. It should have a light crust on the surface and be heated all the way through. You can eat it by itself or chop it up for use in salads, quiche, or soup. And it's wonderful for breakfast, lunch, or dinner.

061

Shank Roast (also known as Ham Shank)

028

This is essentially the other end of a ham, farther down the leg. It is all muscle, with a lot of connective tissue, which is why many people avoid this cut. But if cooked carefully, it's a winner that can be had for very little cost.

What to look for: A shank roast is essentially a special-order item, so you'll need to get it through a butcher. Keeping the cut moist and tender during cooking is essential, so buy a shank roast with the skin on and an even layer of fat. The roast should be 1½ to 2½ lb [680 g to 1.2 kg].

How to cook it: Some ham shanks are sold "ready to eat"—in other words, precooked. I prefer to buy mine fresh. Although you need to cook a shank roast a long time, usually about 6 hours, the result is worth the effort. And cooking it yourself means you control the flavorings and seasonings. I pop mine in the slow cooker before heading out for the day. I add at least 4 cups [960 ml] of low-sodium vegetable broth, a few spices, and sturdy vegetables like carrots and potatoes. Then I let the roast cook all day and come home to an incredibly delicious pork dinner.

Ham Hock (also known as Pork Knuckle)

029

Hock is just another name for "joint," and that's what this is: the front and back leg joints separating the top of the leg from the foot. Hock isn't easy to cook—the cut is filled with connective tissue, which has to be broken down. But as Southern cooks have long known, the cut rewards skillful handling with a distinctive, one-of-a-kind flavor.

What to look for: Go shopping for ham hocks when you're feeling adventurous and want something different. Depending on the recipe you're following, you can find fresh (uncooked) ham hocks and smoked hocks. The cut should include the skin, and the skin should be a light tan. A dark gray or black bone, or marrow that is discolored and mushy, are signs that the hock has been frozen and you should pass on it.

How to cook it: All the connective tissue translates to long cooking time in abundant liquid. Ham hocks are traditionally added to soups and stews and are regularly cooked for hours. The flavor pairs well with traditional soul-food staples such as black-eyed peas and collard greens.

Smoked Shank

This is the bottom of the leg—the shinbone. Although it is mostly muscle and connective tissue, it is unrivaled as a flavoring ingredient. The shank is meatier than the hock, with an abundance of marrow inside that adds a distinctive rich, smoky flavor.

What to look for: As with all smoked cuts, the darker the outside is, the stronger the smoky flavor will be. I prefer smoked shanks that are medium to dark brown. Avoid any that are yellow or are more yellow than brown, which means the shank was not properly smoked and the meat will not be fully cured and may be raw.

How to cook it: I add a smoked shank to split-pea soup; it makes the best split pea soup you'll ever taste. Add the shank to the soup pot when you start the soup, and strip the meat from the bone when you're ready to serve it.

063

LAMB

As a butcher and a meat lover, I believe that lamb is underappreciated in this country. It has never been as popular in the United States as it is in Britain and throughout Europe. That's partly due to America's long history as the world's leading beef producer, and partly a consequence of the climate and terrain in most of Europe, which is better suited for raising sheep than steers. The fact is, Americans eat less than 1 lb [455 g] of lamb annually—about one-hundredth of the amount of chicken we consume. That should change.

Part of the problem is that people often associate lamb with the heavy, gamey flavor of mutton. But lamb is lighter, cleaner, and sweeter than mutton. United States lamb is lighter and sweeter still; U.S. producers finish lamb on grain, while foreign producers usually feed lamb grass throughout the animal's life. A grain diet results in more fat throughout the animal, which gives American lamb a lighter flavor more akin to beef. The extra fat also makes the cuts easier to cook and keeps them from drying out. You'll have the most luck shopping for American lamb at butcher shops and high-end grocery stores.

That said, when supermarkets stock lamb, they tend to carry imported meat, which is more economical and is usually frozen, rather than fresh. Most lamb sold in the United States comes from Australia or New Zealand. Lambs from Down Under tend to be smaller (which means buying a whole leg is more manageable), with a wilder flavor that some might describe as slightly gamey. Even the larger American lambs, when butchered, yield far less meat than a steer, which is why lamb has traditionally been more expensive than beef and is considered a specialty meat for holidays and special occasions.

More recently, though, high beef prices and an increase in lamb imports are forcing the price of lamb down, more into parity with the cost of beef. That's why you're more likely to find lamb on offer in the meat case of your local supermarket or butcher.

Regardless of where you buy it, lamb differs based on the age of the slaughtered animal. A **hothouse lamb** is a baby lamb, usually 6 to 8 weeks old. A **lamb** is any sheep less than 1 year old at slaughter. **Hoggets** are sheep between 1 and 2 years old, and **mutton** are sheep older than 2 years.

True lamb meat should be medium reddish purple, firm, and fine grained. A deep, dark purple indicates an older animal that will be tougher and gamier. If the meat appears extremely dark with yellowish fat or redness on the underside of the rib bones, it is likely mutton being sold as lamb.

065

Ray's ADVICE

I recommend shoppers cook lamb as soon as they get it home. If that's not realistic, carefully store the meat in its original wrapping in the coldest part of your refrigerator—usually on a lower shelf toward the back. Lamb meat deteriorates quickly, but stored correctly it will keep for 3 to 4 days. However, the flavor may become increasingly gamey. If you want to make sure your lamb doesn't taste gamey, freeze it immediately, then thaw it in the refrigerator before cooking.

Industrially raised lambs and imported lambs are available throughout the year. But increasingly, smaller local operations are raising heritage varieties with slightly different flavor profiles. Lamb meat raised on small local farms—especially when the animal has been pastured for its entire life—is best when purchased in season, which is late spring to early fall.

Don't worry if you don't find a grade on the lamb. Grading is voluntary, so many cuts don't even carry one. Although there are five grades of lamb, only two are sold at retail: **USDA Prime** and **USDA Choice.** Prime is better, but the difference is not really noticeable.

A lamb usually breaks down to less than 50 lb [22.7 kg] of meat, so if you and your family like lamb, and you have a large freezer, you might consider buying a whole animal. You can have your butcher break it down into cuts that you can freeze for meals throughout the year.

Lamb primals echo the structure of a steer; they include the **chuck, rib, loin,** and **leg.**

Ground Lamb (not pictured)

Many different cuts on the animal can be ground, but the most marbled—and consequently the most moist—comes from the shoulder.

What to look for: I only buy lamb ground from shoulder meat, because it is the most flavorful. If possible, have your lamb ground fresh, because the meat dries out quickly. Freeze it as soon as you get home if you are not going to use it the same day. It will go bad in less than 48 hours in the refrigerator. Look for ground lamb that is light brown with a texture like modeling clay.

How to cook it: When using ground lamb to make patties or meatballs, try not to handle it too much. Although it's flavorful in its own right, ground lamb marries perfectly with strong herbal flavors, especially rosemary. You can use ground lamb just as you would ground beef, but try classic lamb dishes, such as shepherd's pie, or make your own version of the a classic Greek gyro.

CHUCK

The lamb chuck consists of the **shoulder, foreshank** (also known as **lamb shank**), and the **neck.** This is the most marbled section of a lamb, making the meat juicy and full of flavor. That said, cuts from the shoulder are not especially tender, which is why they are often cooked in liquid for a long time at a low temperature.

Stew Meat (not pictured)

Lamb stew is a way to have delicious and tender lamb without being overwhelmed by the flavor of the meat—you control the spices and other ingredients that will create the flavor profile. Cooking in liquid will also lessen the gamey flavor.

067

What to look for: I prefer to cut stew meat from the shoulder. Because the size of the shoulder makes it harder to cut enough usable cubes, many butchers use leg of lamb (which also makes great kebabs). Either way, just as with beef and veal stew meat, you're looking for a bargain because the cooking will tenderize meat from tougher cuts. Be careful, though, when the label says "lamb neck for stew"; even though it may look meaty in the package, it is just the neck bone with meat left on it—not solid cubes of meat.

How to cook it: I like to sear my lamb stew meat very quickly on all sides before stewing. This helps lock in the moisture and makes for incredibly tender stewed lamb—especially if you start with shoulder meat.

Shoulder Blade Chops (also known as Shoulder Chops)

031

Given their location close to the delicious rib rack, it's no wonder these are the most flavorful lamb chops. However, they are less tender than other lamb chops and will require a bit more prep work and thoughtful cooking to be served at their best.

What to look for: The good news is that these chops are cheaper than rib chops, and when cooked right I think they're every bit as good. Shoulder blade chops should be thicker than rib chops, with nice graining (fine marbling). The meat should be lighter in color than other lamb cuts.

How to cook it: Although some people grill or panfry these chops, I don't suggest it. Unlike rib or loin chops, shoulder blade chops contain connective tissue that has to be broken down if the chop is going to be tender. That means slow cooking is best. Brine or marinate the chops first, and then braise them for a long time—up to 1 hour.

068

Shoulder Arm Chops (also known as Round Bone Chops)

032

Looking for a bargain in lamb chops but don't want to give up any flavor? Welcome to the shoulder arm chop. These are slightly more expensive than the shoulder blade chop because there are a total of six shoulder arm chops in a lamb, as opposed to twelve shoulder blade chops. The arm chop is leaner, with a stronger flavor.

What to look for: These chops are identified by the round bone in the center of the chop. Look for a very lean cut with extremely slight fat marbling, and meat that is a dark reddish purple. The bone should be pure white, not gray, and perfectly circular. An oblong-shaped bone means the chop was cut at the wrong angle (a common mistake among inexperienced butchers). Improperly cut chops will be chewier than those butchered correctly.

How to cook it: Although you'll find this cut grilled in some restaurants, I personally wouldn't attempt it at home. Instead, I braise the chops in red wine and herbs, or panfry them after a long soak in an acidic marinade.

Shoulder Roast

033

Many shoppers and food enthusiasts consider the lamb shoulder roast a great alternative to leg of lamb. The meat is tremendously sweet, and the cut is easy to cook. You don't have to do much to accent the wonderful natural flavor of this roast.

What to look for: Boneless is the way to go with this roast. The cut is already full of flavor, so the bone won't add much, and shoulder bones are hard to carve around when the roast is cooked. You'll inevitably wind up with a lot of wasted meat stuck to the bone.

How to cook it: Want to make lamb shoulder roast to die for? Take a page out of Jamie Oliver's book and preheat the oven to 475°F [240°C]. Dress a 4½-lb [2-kg] roast with unpeeled garlic cloves, bunches of fresh rosemary, and a drizzle of extra-virgin olive oil. Put the meat in the oven, lower the temperature to 325°F [165°C], and roast that piece of meat for 4 to 4½ hours. It will fall off the bone, and you'll have some awfully happy people at your dinner table.

069

Foreshank (also known as Lamb Shank)

034

Any recipe listing "lamb shank" is referring to the foreshank. The foreshank is from the front leg, part of the chuck. It's superior to the hind shank, or back leg, because it includes a larger muscle, and consequently holds up better to the long cooking needed to make the cut tender. One of the most affordable lamb cuts due to its heavy muscling, the foreshank is most often used as stew meat, and sometimes as a base for pasta sauce.

What to look for: You should have no problem finding lamb foreshanks because they are not as sought-after as other lamb cuts. The exception is during Passover, when the foreshank is in high demand. In any case, make sure you're buying the foreshank, and not the hind shank. The meat on the foreshank is about the same thickness from one end to the other, while the hind shank meat tapers, making that cut look more like a drumstick.

How to cook it: Marinate the foreshank in an acidic marinade, such as one with a citrus or red wine base. Then braise it in about 3 cups [720 ml] of chicken or vegetable stock for about 1½ hours.

Lamb Neck

035

This is a little-known cut, which accounts for its very low price. It is sold, usually through a butcher, both with the bone in and without it. Boned, it's often called "neck fillet." Either way, you'll need to tenderize the meat because it's some of the toughest on the animal.

070

What to look for: I buy bone-in lamb neck and use it for a simple stew. It may look like you're not getting a lot of meat, but there is much more than you might think. If possible, buy lamb neck from a butcher or a store that still cuts the full neck bone off of fresh hanging lamb. If you buy from a butcher, request that he butterfly the meat on the neck, leaving it connected to the bone, and cut the bones into 1- to 1½-in [2.5- to 4-cm] pieces.

How to cook it: This is the perfect cut for a slow-cooker stew. Combine about 2 lb [910 g] in a slow cooker with potatoes, carrots, and onions. Add sturdy herbs along with 3 to 4 cups [720 to 960 ml] of vegetable broth. Cook for about 6 hours and enjoy!

RIB

As you might imagine from the name, this primal is essentially the midsection of the animal. This is the section from which the rack of lamb and breast of lamb are cut. While intact, they form what looks like a big bracelet. The rib section has the most marbling of any part of the lamb, making cuts from this section exceedingly tender and flavorful.

Rib Chops

036

Of the three lamb chops—shoulder, rib and loin—the rib chop is the most well marbled. It is closer to a beef texture and flavor than any other lamb cut. The center of the rib chop meat is a tender rib-eye muscle, surrounded by moisturizing and flavor-rich fat.

What to look for: Shop carefully because lamb rib chops can be a bit spendy. The meat should be dark reddish purple and firm to the touch. The outer fat should be white and solid, with fine marbling around and through the eye of each chop. The underside of the bone should have a nearly transparent white membrane and white to light-gray bone. There should be a faint red line running about halfway down the bone, which should look slightly moist. That line is an age indicator. If it's dark and runs farther down the bone, the chop was taken from an older animal.

How to cook it: Lamb rib chops are suitable for cooking in many ways, but I suggest grilling them. Unlike a lot of leaner lamb cuts, the rib chop does well on the grill. Cook it over high heat to start—just until the outside is seared—and then finish it over medium heat. Watch the chops closely, the meat should be cooked medium-rare for optimum flavor and tenderness.

071

Ray's ADVICE

One of the wonderful things about lamb is that there is a cut, flavor, and presentation for just about any occasion. Here are my recommendations for the cuts that will make your next cookout or birthday a truly special event.

Gourmet cookout: Rib Chops (page 071). You won't find a better grilling chop on any animal, and it's quick and easy to cook.

Celebration for a special day: Rack of Lamb (below). The delicious meat and large portions that can quickly be cut into individual servings make rack of lamb a great choice for birthday parties or other special occasions.

Holiday made memorable: Crown Roast (facing page). This is a classic centerpiece for the holiday table. The meat is delicious, and the presentation is an elegant show in itself.

Weeknight wonderful: Shoulder Roast (page 069). Pop it in a slow cooker with potatoes and veggies and 3 to 4 cups [720 to 960 ml] of water before you head out to work and come home to a delicious, filling meal ready to go on the table.

072

037

Rack of Lamb

This cut is perpendicular to the spine, and usually includes the ribs on one side—eight in total. The rack is composed of rib chops, which are cut into separate servings after the rack is cooked. The advantage is that the rack will shrink less and hold more flavor than chops cooked individually. It is also easier to cook one large piece instead of eight individual chops. If you're looking to feed a crowd, you can buy the complete rack—sold as a double rack—with sixteen ribs. The double rack is usually cooked like a roast.

What to look for: I don't buy Frenched rack of lamb because I don't want to lose the extra meat. However, if you're throwing a fancy dinner party or plating the rack for a special occasion, a Frenched rack looks very elegant and special. Have the butcher French the rack and ask him to crack the chine (the backbone) between the ribs if that hasn't already been done. Whenever you're shopping for rack of lamb, the fat across the top should be evenly trimmed, rather than thicker on one side or the other.

How to cook it: A rack of lamb is best cooked medium-rare. The classic way of preparing the cut is with a simple rub of fresh rosemary and garlic, a light seasoning of salt and pepper, and a drizzle of olive oil. Let the rack come to room temperature and put it in a 425°F [220°C] oven. Cook it for about 7 minutes, and then lower the temperature to 325°F [165°C] and cook for 8 to 10 minutes more. Check the lamb by inserting an instant-read thermometer into the meat without hitting a bone. When it reads 145°F [63°C], the rack is medium-rare. Remove it from the oven and let rest for about 10 minutes before serving.

Crown Roast

038

Although pork crown roast is popular, the original and authentic crown roast is made with lamb, which provides a deeper, richer flavor than any pig can offer. The crown is the product of butchering skill, rather than a specific cut, since it is made with the rack of lamb. A single rack of lamb serves two people. The crown roast, which is made from at least two racks, will feed a bigger crowd and makes a festive presentation. The racks of lamb are tied together and then bent into a circle. The bones are Frenched so that they stick up like the spikes on a crown. Although it's possible to form the crown roast at home, having a butcher do it for you guarantees success.

073

What to look for: A good crown roast is made of racks that are all exactly the same size, so that they match up correctly when the crown is tied. This will also ensure proper and even cooking. The chine bone needs to be cracked between each rib just enough so that it flexes, but not so much that the rib meat eye is cut.

How to cook it: Crown roasts are almost always slow roasted. I cook mine at 350°F [180°C] for 2½ hours. Before you put the crown in the oven, cover all the exposed rib bones with aluminum foil to keep them from turning black during cooking. The center is traditionally filled with stuffing before serving. The stuffing can be cooked in the oven while the crown roasts or made on the stove top.

Breast

039

Sold with the bone in or boneless, the breast is the underside of the lamb bracelet. It's some of the least expensive lamb, and some of the least expensive meat—period. The meat requires slow cooking, but get it right and it's delectable.

What to look for: The meat on the breast should be pale pink, and the fat should be firm and white, never gray. Because the breast has less meat than other lamb cuts, I strongly recommend buying a boneless lamb breast and stuffing it with freshly ground lamb. The cut is already inexpensive, so you won't save much with a bone-in breast. The ground lamb will absorb the great flavor from the fat of the breast and make for a heartier roast that will feed more people.

074

How to cook it: Although some people grill lamb breast, I think it tastes best cooked as a roast. I put mine in a slow cooker with chicken broth, carrots, garlic, and onions and cook it all day. Do it this way, and you'll enjoy melt-in-your-mouth meat when you get home from work.

Riblets

040

Riblets are short pieces cut off the breast ends of the ribs. They may look like afterthoughts, but they are delicious and easy to cook. They are also relatively inexpensive and a great bargain.

What to look for: I prefer my riblets fresh cut. The meat can dry out if stored for even a few days. Look for a nice creamy white layer of fat lining the riblets. That layer will keep them moist and flavorful during cooking.

How to cook it: Riblets can be cooked many different ways, but I prefer to braise them in wine for an hour or so. You will wind up with meat that is almost falling off the bone and so delectable that you'll wish you had bought more riblets.

LOIN

What most customers and butchers call a "lamb loin" is actually half a loin. The full loin is called the **saddle** and includes both side loins, the flank meat that runs through the loin section, and the portion of the back that connects them. The loin is meaty, tender, relatively lean, and full of flavor. It has a T-shaped bone running through it, separating the loin meat from the fillet, just as in a porterhouse steak. Consequently, it is broken down into some of the priciest lamb cuts. The most popular are **loin chops.** However, the loin yields a wonderful roast and other interesting cuts.

Loin Chops

075

041

Butchers and other professionals are fond of saying these are the lamb's porterhouse cut. That's because they are thick, full of flavor, and cook like that popular steak. But I think the lamb is sweeter and has a more unique flavor than the beefy porterhouse. In any case, this is a sizable chop with lots of flavorful meat to satisfy the biggest appetite.

What to look for: The thicker lamb loin chops are, the better. I like mine cut 2 in [5 cm] thick. You should see light to moderate marbling, but no big areas of fat. The fat should all be creamy white and firm. The fillet meat on the underside of the bone should be at least ½ in [12 mm] wide.

How to cook it: These are the lamb chops I would choose to grill, although many people like to broil them. Either way, season them liberally with salt and pepper and let them come to room temperature before cooking. They are absolutely spectacular grilled to medium-rare over high heat and then served with a nice arugula pesto or mint chimichurri.

076

Loin Roast

042

When it comes to lamb, this is the premier roast. It will run you a pretty penny, but the meat is purely delicious and the cut is ideal for a crowd. The loin roast is sold with the bone in or boned and rolled, which is easier for the home cook to handle. You'll pay more for the boned-and-rolled version.

What to look for: I much prefer a boned-and-rolled loin roast. You may save a little money with a bone-in roast, but after trying to slice all the meat off the bone you may find that it's not quite the value it seemed to be at first. The roast should have firm, white fat covering at least ¼ in [6 mm] thick.

How to cook it: The loin's strong flavor does well roasted or grilled. I prefer to rub it with salt, pepper, minced garlic, and rosemary and then roast it at 375°F [190°C] for 30 to 35 minutes for medium-rare (145°F [63°C]).

Noisettes (not pictured)

These are lamb loin chops that have been boned and then rolled into tight little rounds. Noisettes are perfect single servings, although they are so small that two are often served per plate. For tenderness and flavor, the noisette is on par with the filet mignon—a truly elegant, decadent meal.

What to look for: Properly prepared noisettes should include a nice ring of fat all the way around the cut, which will help keep the meat moist during cooking and will add flavor.

How to cook it: Noisettes can be grilled or roasted, but I prefer to pan-sear mine. I give them about 2 minutes per side to get a nice char on the surface. Then I finish them under the broiler, about 6 in [15 cm] away from the heat. Noisettes are traditionally cooked simply, seasoned with rosemary, lemon, and garlic.

077

Lamb Tenderloin

043

All tenderloin cuts are known for their tenderness and mild flavor. They are also the leanest cut from any animal. Add to that combination the rich flavor of lamb, and the tenderloin is pure gold. It will be hard to find, but well worth the search.

What to look for: Pick out lamb tenderloin that is light red with absolutely no apparent moisture in the package. Or better yet, get your tenderloin from a butcher who buys Certified Humane lambs.

How to cook it: Lamb tenderloin is fantastic for grilling or pan-searing. I like to coat the tenderloin with a layer of olive oil and cover it with a spice rub. Sear it in a pan for a few minutes on each side, until a nice crust forms, and you'll have a delectable, healthful dinner.

LEG

Leg of lamb is a favorite throughout Mediterranean countries, where the whole leg is often roasted with regional herbs. Because the lamb is a relatively small animal, the entire primal is a manageable piece of meat for special occasions, when you're feeding a large crowd. It can be cooked several different ways and is hard to ruin. It is also broken down into boneless cuts that can be stuffed or cooked and served in a number of different ways, including bone-in portions that make wonderful meals similar to bone-in roasts but with a much more delicate and distinctive flavor.

Leg of Lamb

044

Leg of lamb is the most efficient and economical cut to serve a group, and it's ideal for roasting. Although a whole leg might sound daunting, keep in mind that the average lamb is much smaller than the average steer or pig. A leg of lamb is a totally reasonable meal, one that has historically been served as an Easter specialty. It serves six nicely, and any leftover meat will be delicious for sandwiches or salads a day or two later. It's also one of the cheapest lamb cuts you can buy, with no lack of flavor. The leg is sold bone-in or boneless, and you'll often find boneless legs conveniently stuffed, rolled, and tied, complete with cooking instructions. A boneless leg can also be left flat for grilling, although you'll need a large grill. A bone-in leg is usually butchered to either the sirloin side or the round side. The sirloin side is more common because it features slightly more meat and is more tender.

What to look for: Best to go to a butcher you trust for this cut. You'll want the leg properly dressed (cut and trimmed), and if you are roasting the lamb, you should have the butcher remove the hip bone, making the cut semiboneless. This will make it easier to

078

carve. A lamb leg should weigh no more than 9 lb [4 kg]. If it weighs more, you may be buying mutton. The leg should have a light layer of fat, thinning as it runs back toward the shank.

How to cook it: When it comes to leg of lamb, there is no equal to roasting. Prepare the meat with just a simple dry rub of a few spices and then roast the leg dry.

Shank Half Leg

045

This is the bottom half of the leg of lamb, which tapers down to, and includes, the hind shank, or back leg. This cut is best when a whole leg is too much but you still want an elegant presentation on the table. The shank half leg will feed four.

What to look for: The meatiest part of the leg is the middle, so you want to make sure to get a true shank half. It should weigh 4 to 4½ lb [1.8 to 2 kg]. The round bone visible in the cut surface of the roast should be no bigger than a dime. If the bone is too large or off to one side, the shank half leg was cut at the wrong angle. The meat should be very lean and dark reddish purple, with a thin, almost transparent fat cover.

How to cook it: Roast this cut after rubbing it with rosemary, garlic, salt, and pepper to bring out the meat's flavor. Slice the meat thin, against the grain, to ensure tenderness.

Butt Half Leg

046

The butt half leg is the upper portion, from the loin and sirloin down through the middle of the leg. This is the more flavorful and tender half of the leg. The drawback to this cut is that it includes the hip bone, which is difficult to carve around and makes for a less elegant presentation than the shank half leg.

What to look for: As with the shank half leg, the meat should be dark reddish purple with a thin cover of white fat across the top. A full butt half leg should weigh 5½ to 6 lb [2.5 to 2.7 kg]. You should see a perfectly round bone in the center of the cut surface, about the size of a dime.

079

How to cook it: Roast the butt half leg just as you would a shank half leg, seasoned with kosher salt and freshly ground black pepper, a bit of minced fresh rosemary if you like, and crushed garlic.

Butterflied Leg

047
Home cooks who would be overwhelmed by a whole leg of lamb will be better served with a butterflied leg. Butterflying makes it easier to season the meat and ensure even cooking. A butterflied leg also requires less cooking time, making this a better choice when you want to spend less time in the kitchen.

What to look for: The meat should be dark reddish purple with a layer of fat on the bottom. Most important, the leg should be butterflied evenly, so that the thickness of the meat is consistent from one side to the other. This ensures the lamb will cook evenly.

How to cook it: One of the best reasons to choose a butterflied leg of lamb is so you can stuff and roll it. In that case, you'll be roasting the cut. If you are planning on grilling the meat, make sure you get a butterflied butt half leg. The sirloin meat will hold up better to the high heat of the grill.

Sirloin Chops

048
This is the cut of choice if you want the true flavor of lamb in a less-expensive chop. The sirloin chop has less bone and more meat than either the loin or rib chop. One chop will feed one very hungry person, or leave leftovers that hold up well to reheating.

080

What to look for: Like other lamb chops, select your sirloin chop based on color. It should be a lovely pink and have moderate, even marbling throughout the cut. Pick the smallest sirloin chops you can find. They will be from a younger animal, and the meat will have a light, appealing flavor.

How to cook it: Make no mistake, this is a grilling chop. There are a lot of panfried recipes out there, but I either throw this on the grill outdoors or use a grill pan inside. Before you grill the chop, treat it with a simple spice rub and let it come to room temperature.

Sirloin Roast

049

This is just about the perfect roast. Nicely marbled with fat, the meat has a rich flavor. It's also easy to cook this cut to melt-in-your mouth perfection. A sirloin roast is a great alternative to roasting an entire leg because an average sirloin roast is just right for four people (a smaller sirloin roast will serve two nicely). You'll pay a high price for it, but the eating will be well worth whatever you spend.

What to look for: The meat in the sirloin roast should be dark reddish purple, with a thin cover of white fat.

How to cook it: This is a classic roast, and it should be cooked in a classic way. Coat it with a wet rub such as olive oil, minced garlic, salt, and pepper. Cook a 3-lb [1.4-kg] lamb sirloin roast in a 375°F [190°C] oven for about 50 minutes for medium-rare. Let it rest for about 10 minutes and then slice it as thin as possible.

Leg Steak

050

A lamb leg steak is a way of having the rich-flavored goodness of a leg in a handy, single-serving portion. It is cut from the dead-center meatiest part of the leg of lamb. Resembling a ham steak, it is extremely lean with just a little round bone in the middle. This steak is easy to cook and reasonably priced.

What to look for: A leg steak should be dark reddish purple. It should have a very thin layer of fat running about three-quarters of the way around the edge, and a small, round bone in the middle. If the bone is off to one side avoid the steak; it was cut too far back on the leg.

How to cook it: You don't have to do much to make a delicious meal from a leg steak. Rub it all over with a mixture of minced garlic and fresh rosemary, and then panfry the steak for 3 minutes per side.

081

051

Cutlets

Among lamb eaters, cutlets are popular for their versatility, and they are also kid-friendly. They are economical because serving cutlets is more about the number of pieces than about the overall weight. Unlike chicken and veal cutlets, the flavor of a lamb cutlet is strong and will hold up to even heavily seasoned breading. The best lamb cutlets come from the leg, because leg meat is lean and flavorful and will be tender when sliced thin for cutlets.

What to look for: Lamb cutlets should be evenly colored a nice reddish purple and should be no thicker than ⅛ in [4 mm]. A lamb cutlet must be cut against the grain to be tender, so you want to see a crisscross pattern on the surface of the meat. Lines running in one direction across the meat means it has been cut with the grain and will be tough no matter how you cook it. Buy one or two cutlets per person.

How to cook it: All lamb cutlets need is a little seasoning and breading and they're ready to be panfried. Mix flour with your favorite seasonings, such as garlic salt and freshly ground black pepper, in one shallow dish. Put seasoned bread crumbs in another dish, and lightly beaten eggs in a third. Coat each cutlet in the flour, dip it in the eggs, and press the cutlet into the seasoned bread crumbs until it is coated on both sides. Panfry for 2 minutes per side. Lamb cutlets are also great as leftovers. With a little mint jelly spread on top, the cutlet turns an everyday sandwich into a gourmet lunch.

082

THE STRONGER SIDE OF LAMB

Although most people prefer lamb with a light flavor, if you like a stronger, gamier taste, you can't go wrong with mutton. Mutton is lamb between the ages of two and five years old. Ideally, you'll want meat from an animal that is closer to two years old. You can get an idea of how old the lamb was by looking at the red in the rib bones. A darker red running farther down the bone indicates an older animal. Cut the chuck into 1½-in [4-cm] cubes.

You'll find a lot of value in this protein, although you'll most likely have to buy it from a butcher because you won't find it in the meat case. Although lamb is available year-round, shop for mutton between October and March; the meat sold then came from animals that had access to summer and fall grasses as they were putting on fat prior to slaughter. That grazing gives the meat a deeper, richer flavor and makes it more tender. Grass-fed mutton, like grass-fed beef, will also be high in omega-3 oils. It will also be lower in saturated fat than beef (but higher in cholesterol). The intensity of the flavor and the higher cholesterol means you should serve slightly smaller portions per person than you would if you were making beef for dinner.

VEAL

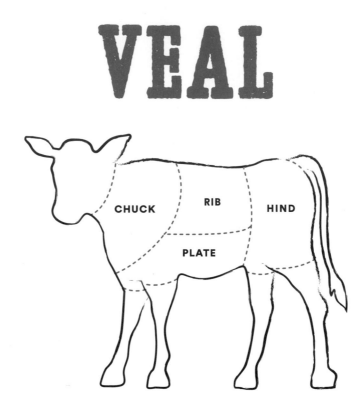

CHUCK RIB HIND

PLATE

Back when I started as a butcher—way before the fantastic selection of packaged meat you'll find in supermarkets now was widely available—veal was a premium, much-sought-after product. It was the butcher's crown jewel. The meat of the wealthy in ancient Rome, veal has long been a favorite in European fine dining. So it should come as no surprise that only the most skilled butchers were traditionally allowed to work on veal. It was a point of pride the first time I butchered a calf.

Veal became popular with the introduction of milk-fed calves who weren't exposed to grain or grain-based feeds. Due to a lack of iron, the meat was white, sweet, and remarkably tender. It was considered a gourmet food best suited to special occasions. It was also the most expensive meat you could buy.

But a few bad producers who used inhumane processes to raise the animals gave veal a bad name. Fortunately, the USDA has been able to turn the situation around by instituting tighter regulations regarding pen size and treatment standards for calves prior to slaughter. The organic community has also raised veal's profile by raising calves with access to pastures and adding grain to their diet, resulting in more flavorful meat, often called "pink veal." It's now easier than ever to find veal labeled Certified Humane, which have been certified by Humane Farm Animal Care. These days, veal is getting a new reputation as the lower-cost, low-fat alternative to beef.

FINDING AND COOKING YOUR VEAL

If you're after the more traditional product, you'll want to look for creamy white meat. If you're shopping for partially grain-fed veal, look for light pink meat.

In either case, buy thicker cuts and cut them down as necessary. Thinner cuts of veal dry out quickly. Veal is most often sautéed, like the thinly sliced scaloppine, or braised, which is the case for thicker chops and roasts. Veal chops are also grilled. Regardless of how you prepare your veal, most cuts are best cooked to medium (160°F [71°C])—the point at which it is still moist and is most flavorful.

Veal is calf meat and, although it's the same animal, the smaller calf is sectioned differently than an adult steer. The sections are not referred to as "primals," but the idea is the same—identifying major sections from which individual cuts are taken. The **foreshank** and **hind shank** are the front and back legs, respectively. The other sections of a veal calf are, from front to back, **chuck, plate, rib, and hind.**

085

Ground Veal (not pictured)

The naturally delicate nature and lower-fat content of veal makes for wonderful ground meat. The meat is normally ground fine. It should be used the day you buy it, and should be cooked carefully to avoid drying it out.

What to look for: Because ground veal does not age well in the package, you probably won't find it in a supermarket meat case. It's best to get it from a butcher. Ask the butcher to grind a package of veal stew, or grind the veal stew yourself. Always freeze ground veal as soon as you get home if you're not going to use it right away.

How to cook it: Ground veal can be used in any recipe that calls for ground beef; just expect the flavor to be lighter and milder. That's why I don't use ground veal for burgers. But if you season veal as you would pork sausage, it can be a great low-fat alternative in any dish made with sausage. I think ground veal shines when it's used in combination with other meats, for example to make meat loaf or meatballs. Its lean nature will lower the total fat content and add a little sweetness to the other meats. Use equal parts ground veal, beef, and pork for a really good flavor.

CHUCK

Veal chuck yields many flavorful cuts, which are generally less tender than other parts of the calf. They are also the least expensive. Cutlets, for example, are usually cut from the shoulder. They have a little more flavor but are tougher than those cut from the hind leg, such as the traditional thinly sliced **scaloppine.**

086

052

Shoulder Chops (also known as Shoulder Blade Chops)

These chops usually come with the bone in and are cut from the neck. You can find boneless versions, however, which are called boneless chuck. For most recipes, they are interchangeable. Either way, this is a kosher cut. Keeping kosher involves using only the front of the animal. Although these are not the most tender of chops, they can be very flavorful if cooked right.

What to look for: I buy bone-in chops and look to the bone as a sign of quality. The color should range from white to light gray.

How to cook it: I prefer to marinate my veal shoulder chops and grill them over low heat, which can really bring out the best in the meat. Always finish a veal chop with some type of fat—I use olive oil, but some people use butter or even bone marrow.

Round Bone Chops

053

Round bone chops are cut from the shoulder side of the neck, and get their name from the round bone that runs through it. Unlike shoulder chops, these actually include the meat from the shoulder. Although they are leaner and much meatier than shoulder chops, the cooking method is the same. These chops are more expensive and harder to find than shoulder chops, because there are only four good round bone chops in a calf.

What to look for: Pay attention to the round bone in the chop; it should be whiter than a typical beef bone. The marrow in the center of the bone should be about the size of a dime. If the marrow is too small, it's an indication that the bone is bigger on the bottom of the chop, making that chop less desirable.

How to cook it: Like all chuck cuts, this one calls for slow, moist, penetrating cooking. I like to simmer this lean cut in a deep saucepan with about 2 in [5 cm] of wine, which reduces to a really nice sauce. The wine works well with the taste of veal, and it ensures that the veal stays moist.

087

Shoulder Roast (also known as Clod Roast)

054

The shoulder is one of the larger veal roasts. It is usually sold boneless, which is the best way to buy it. This roast is generally cheaper and thicker, with more of a fat covering than other veal roasts. That makes it a great choice to feed a large crowd, and is why it is a kosher holiday favorite. You will also find the shoulder roast cut up for veal stew.

What to look for: Because this lean cut will shrink more than beef does, I allow 8 oz [230 g] per person. There should be some fat covering the roast, which should be soft, white, and opaque—not translucent. If you can see the meat through the fat cover, the roast is old and has lost a lot of moisture.

How to cook it: Because this is from the tougher section of a calf, you want to break down the meat during cooking. I recommend roasting a 4½- to 5-lb [2- to 2.3-kg] clod roast for about 1 hour in a 350°F [180°C] oven. Add 3 cups [720 ml] of chicken or beef stock or wine to the pan and baste the roast with the liquid.

Shoulder Cutlets

055

Veal cutlets are thinly sliced pieces of veal. Although they are often taken from the back leg or round, cutlets from the shoulder are priced lower and will have slightly more flavor. They are also a little tougher. You can find packaged shoulder cutlets that have been pounded thin, so that they resemble scaloppine. The pounding tenderizes the cutlet. If the label includes only the words "veal cutlets," what's inside may have been sliced from anywhere on the animal.

What to look for: Buy boneless cutlets, as fresh as possible. In fact, it's worth finding a butcher to slice the cutlets to order. The fresher they are, the better the flavor, and the more the cut will retain veal's natural tenderness and moisture. Shoulder cutlets will be white to light pink in color and slightly darker than cutlets from the leg. (Those taken from the hind leg or round are lighter and are labeled "veal cutlets from the leg.")

How to cook it: I'm Italian, so I'm biased; there is nothing like a veal cutlet pounded thin and breaded with flour, lightly beaten eggs, and seasoned bread crumbs (in that order). Drop the cutlet in hot olive oil, cook for about 3 minutes on each side, and you have a restaurant-quality dinner that should be served with nothing more than a small pile of marinara-coated pasta and lemon wedges.

Chuck Roast

056

This veal roast is more tender than a beef chuck roast and has a lot less fat, which makes it an ideal substitute in many recipes. Veal chuck roast is typically sold boneless and tied with twine. Because the tied roast is thick, which helps it cook more evenly throughout, it remains juicy and flavorful. This is especially important with a meat as lean as veal.

What to look for: A small "petite" veal chuck roast, about 2 lb [910 g], will serve two people perfectly. For a family, choose a 4-lb [1.8-kg] roast.

How to cook it: Roast for about 1 hour in a 350°F [180°C] oven with 3 to 4 cups [720 to 960 ml] of beef stock or another salty braising liquid, which will flavor as well as tenderize the meat. I also add potatoes and veggies and cook this just like a pot roast.

Stew Meat (not pictured)

The wonderful thing about using veal for stew meat is that the light, pale meat soaks up the other flavors. Good veal stew meat can be cut from the shoulder, but meat from the chuck is your best bet. It is the only meat in veal with a hint of fat running through it, so it will hold up better to longer cooking and add more flavor to your stew.

089

What to look for: Avoid precut veal stew meat, which is generally made from small pieces of meat left over from other cuts. You'll end up with veal trimmings and not solid veal cubes. It's best to have a piece of boneless chuck or boneless shoulder cut into stew meat for you. The meat should be cut into uniform, 2-in [5-cm] cubes—a little larger than beef stew meat, to keep the leaner veal from drying out. Plan on using the meat immediately (or freeze it as soon as you get home).

How to cook it: A rich wine-and-butter-based recipe is especially good with this type of stew meat. Because the cubes will be tougher than meat from other parts of the calf, you'll want to give the meat a long cooking time and plenty of liquid. Strong flavors, like rosemary and garlic, and sturdy vegetables are the perfect partners for the stew pot.

PLATE

The plate is the chest of the calf. It is a simple section, producing only two cuts. But both can be rewarding pieces of meat when used to their best advantage in recipes.

Breast and Brisket

057

090

Brisket is the largest piece of meat taken from the breast and is sold boneless. Whole breast is sold bone-in or boneless. The brisket meat runs through only half the breast, but it accounts for most of the meat. Veal breast can be a bit of a challenge to cook, because it ranges over its length from stringy and tough to a little bit fatty. Unlike some other veal cuts, the breast or brisket, like the shoulder, will hold up to a long cooking time in the oven without drying out; when stuffed, it can feed a big crowd.

What to look for: It's most likely that you'll need to order this cut from a butcher. When ordering a breast, you need to be explicit; it can vary in size from 5 to 15 lb [2.3 to 6.8 kg], depending on the age of the calf. Veal brisket is extremely lean and runs 4 to 6 lb [1.8 to 2.7 kg]. Because the cut is much easier to work with and

cooks relatively quickly, I buy the brisket. With a little careful braising, veal brisket can be as tender and flavorful as any other cut on
the calf. It will shrink a lot, though. Figure ¾ lb [340 g] per person.

How to cook it: You can go fancy or plain with a veal breast or
brisket. You need to keep the meat from drying out, which is why
any recipe featuring veal breast or brisket includes at least 4 cups
[960 ml] of liquid, most often wine or broth. You can stuff the
brisket with a wet stuffing, which will help keep the meat moist.
In the traditional French style of cooking the breast, called veal
breast confit, the fat is rendered and then used to cook the vegetables and meat. This requires a lot of time and effort, but the result
is a special-occasion dish. The brisket is usually browned and then
braised or roasted for about 1½ hours, which is a lot less time than
a beef brisket would take.

RIB

This midsection has the most fat of any part of the animal, making
the rib area the most flavorful part. Start with the namesake ribs,
which are sectioned off into separate pieces that cook and eat quite
differently and have tons of potential for cooks. The tender roasts
that come from this part of the animal make incredibly delicious,
lean alternatives to traditional beef roasts. And, of course, there are
also the veal chops that are such a steakhouse favorite. Those chops
are reason enough to fire up the grill and create an unforgettable
meal. All of this is why the rib section is one of my favorites on this
and the other animals.

091

Rib Chops

058

Rib chops have the light, sweet flavor of veal and, because they
are from the rib, are the juiciest of veal chops. This cut is also easy
to cook and can be served as an elegant main course, a wonderful
starter, or a low-fat alternative for the grill. Although they are on
the pricey side, most meat eaters feel that these chops are well
worth the expense.

What to look for: Veal rib chops should ideally be ¾ to 1 in [2 to 2.5 cm] thick. The thickness will help the cut retain its flavor and moisture when cooked, and makes a chop a perfect portion size for one person. The bones should be a whitish gray and the meat should be white to light pink, and slightly firm. (Very soft veal is a sign of excessive water, which points to mishandling in the production chain.)

How to cook it: There is almost no wrong way to cook veal rib chops; they can be broiled, grilled or—the way I prefer—pan-roasted. I sear them about 4 minutes per side over medium-high heat, then slide the chops, pan and all, into a 450°F [230°C] oven for about 10 minutes for medium (160°F [71°C]).

059

Rack of Veal

A rack of veal comprises the first six ribs in the rib cage. This is the same cut as a beef prime rib. It is the most flavorful and tender cut in a calf. Although it is, in fact, the rib chops connected in one piece, a rack of veal is cooked like a roast. Its size protects the meat during cooking, so that the rack ends up being more flavorful than individual chops. It shrinks less as well.

What to look for: The size of the rack and of the individual chops varies with the age of the calf. That means you'll find racks ranging from 5 to 6½ lb [2.3 to 3 kg], which is enough for four adults, while larger ones weigh 6 to 8 lb [2.7 to 3.6 kg].

How to cook it: Roasting is by far the preferred method for cooking a rack of veal. The tender and mild meat comes to life when treated with a spice rub prior to cooking.

092

060

Rib-Eye Roast (also known as Veal Fillet)

This is boneless rack of veal, which most stores sell under the name veal fillet. It is very expensive and not as easy to cook as a rack of veal. Without the bone, the meat is prone to dry out more quickly and shrink more. The only advantage to this cut over the rack of veal is that you don't have to deal with the bones.

What to look for: A rib-eye roast will be 3 to 4 in [7.5 to 10 cm] longer than a rack of veal because the roast is cut with more than just the first six ribs, going farther into the chuck. This translates to a little more flavor. The meat should be white to light pink and should be firm. The weight ranges from 2 to 4 lb [910 to 1.8 kg].

How to cook it: Roast this cut and baste it regularly as it cooks. I use a rich sauce, like a wine-and-butter sauce, for basting the roast and keeping it moist.

HIND

The hind section on a calf, also known as **hind saddle**, includes the **rump**, **loin**, and **upper leg**—and a whole lot of good eating. The best steaks on the young animal come from this area, as do some of the most flavorful veal cuts. You'll pay more, but you'll be buying the best veal.

093

Strip Loin

061

This is a hefty boneless cut that offers lots of options in the kitchen. It can be a little pricey but virtually nothing of the cut is wasted, and every bite—when cooked correctly—will just about melt in your mouth. It's a great choice for a large dinner party.

What to look for: I know people lean toward convenience in their meat purchases, but this is a case where I would suggest buying the meat with the strip of fat and silverskin still attached. These help keep the relatively lean meat moist, and you can easily remove them just prior to cooking. The strip loin averages about 4½ lb [2 kg] and feeds six people with leftovers.

How to cook it: This significant piece of meat is often cut down into thick steaks then pan-roasted, although you can stuff the roast and cook it in the oven as you would any roast, to medium (160°F [71°C]), for a super-tender large meal roast.

Porterhouse (also known as Loin Chops)

062

For years, this cut was sold as **loin veal chops.** But the USDA, in an effort to help people better understand what they were buying, has renamed the cut. This makes sense, because it is the one veal cut that will chew like a steak, and it makes a great low-fat alternative to its beef counterpart. On the plate, a veal porterhouse resembles a T-bone, with a long bone separating the tenderloin section on one side and the strip loin section on the other.

What to look for: You simply can't go wrong with a veal porterhouse. The veal rib chop gets more press, but this is just about my favorite cut on the calf. Most of the meat should be off-white to light pink, but the tenderloin on the bottom of the T-shaped bone is always darker in color than the rest of the meat.

How to cook it: Grilling is far and away the preferred method of preparation, and you will get the best flavor by cooking the meat to medium (160°F [71°C]). If you don't have a grill or grill pan handy, you can pan-roast the meat in a cast-iron skillet over high heat.

094

Tenderloin Roast and Medallions

063

The name says it all; this is one of the most tender cuts you'll find on a calf. It is smaller and more manageable than the same cut taken from a steer. A veal tenderloin roast is perfect for a family of four. And you can cut it into medallions yourself.

What to look for: When buying veal tenderloin, be sure that is actually what you're getting. It should be 10 to 14 in [25 to 35.5 cm] long and taper to a point at one end. The cut should not be the same thickness throughout. The meat will be darker than other veal cuts and should be firm to the touch.

How to cook it: The best way to prep the tenderloin is cut it into medallions. Slice each medallion 1¼ to 1½ in [3 to 4 cm] thick. Leave the last 3 in [7.5 cm] of the tapered end whole. Make a cut halfway down the middle of the tapered piece and then open up the two sides to create a butterflied piece the same thickness as the medallions. The trick with veal tenderloin is to not overcook it, which would negate the tenderness of the cut. Never cook a tender-loin roast or medallions past medium (160°F [71°C]).

Sirloin Roast (also known as Veal Rump Roast)

064

Sold bone-in or boneless, the sirloin roast is cut from the rump and, consequently, often sold as veal rump roast. With the bone in, it is often called sirloin standing roast. When boneless, the roast can be found as a single- or double-rolled sirloin roast (for a double-rolled roast, two loins are stacked, rolled, and tied).

095

What to look for: I prefer this roast boneless. The younger bones in veal do not add flavor, as they do in beef. And when you try to cut the meat off the bone, you may lose some of the best-tasting meat in the roast. Given the cost and the natural tendency of lean veal to shrink, you want to make sure to get the most out of the roast when you slice it.

How to cook it: Like other veal roasts, this one should be roasted with at least 3 cups [720 ml] of liquid in the pan to ensure that it doesn't dry out during cooking.

Leg Cutlets

065

Veal leg cutlets are considered an elegant, special-occasion meal, an assumption that is reinforced by the high price tag. Although cutlets can technically be cut from any part of the animal, the best are cut from the hind leg, or round, and they should be sliced against the grain. Cutlets from any other part of the animal will be tougher.

What to look for: Make sure the label indicates that the cutlets are from the hind leg, or round. They should be white to very light pink—noticeably lighter than other veal cuts. All the pieces in the package should be the same size, to make cooking them easy. Stay away from meat with what appears to be lines running through it. This means the cutlets were not sliced against the grain and will be tough, no matter how you cook them. When sliced properly, the surface of the meat should have a faint crisscross pattern.

How to cook it: The best way to cook these cutlets is to bread them and fry them (see Shoulder Cutlets on page 088). Unlike shoulder cutlets, these do not need to be pounded first; they are tender enough. Serve with roasted potatoes and broccoli rabe for a fabulous and fabulously simple meal. The cutlets are also wonderful when served with a wine sauce such as marsala or a simple, sturdy marinara to make parmigiana, served with a side of angel hair pasta.

Scaloppine

066

Scaloppine are more expensive than regular cutlets because the butcher has to use premium veal top round to cut one long, thin slice without butterflying it and still retain some flavor. Because veal is soft and difficult to slice evenly across such a long piece, the slices are pounded paper-thin. This ensures an even thickness across the entire surface of the cut, making it better suited to cooking, and giving it exceptional tenderness. Veal top round has some of the strongest flavor of any cut. And because veal is already naturally tender, slicing this cut so thinly and pounding it takes it from plain tender to melt-in-your-mouth tender.

What to look for: The best scaloppine come from a butcher shop. If you don't have a trusted butcher, you can make the scaloppine yourself. Place a slice of veal top round between two sheets of wax paper and lightly pound the meat with a mallet turned sideways (to increase the surface area of the blow and avoid tearing the meat). Pound lightly from the center out to the left and then to the right, until the meat is an even thickness all the way across its surface.

How to cook it: Veal scaloppine are always cooked quickly. Although they are most often breaded and panfried, they can also be sautéed with butter, lemon, and capers to lightly glaze the meat and add delicate nuance that complement the veal's natural flavor.

Top Round

067

Taken from the top of the rear leg, this is a delicious roast that is so tender it is often sliced into cutlets or scaloppine. The roast itself averages about 4 lb [1.8 kg] and will feed six to eight people.

What to look for: This cut should be white to light pink and firm to the touch.

How to cook it: Roast or braise veal top round. It should be kept protected during cooking with a fat source. That's why it's often roasted in melted butter in a large casserole or wrapped in thinly sliced beef fat.

Round Steak (not pictured)

The round steak is cut from the veal top round, as are scaloppine. The difference between the two cuts is the thickness; round steak is cut ¼ to ½ in [6 to 12 mm] thick.

What to look for: The round steak has a clearly visible, small, round muscle that runs along one side. This muscle gets smaller, disappearing at the back of the cut. The bigger this muscle, the better. A bigger muscle is a sign that the cut was taken from the more desirable front to the center of the top round. One round steak will feed one or two people.

097

How to cook it: The fuller flavor of the top round makes this cut ideal for a quick sauté in wine sauce. But I prefer to bread and fry this cut, much as you would a cutlet. You could also use the breaded steak as a base for a hearty veal parmigiana. It will not hold up to grilling or baking, though, which will dry out the meat and make it tough.

Eye of Round Roast (not pictured)
Coming from the same part of the animal where the best cutlets are sliced, this roast is shaped like a veal tenderloin. It is a little shorter, 8 to 10 in [20 to 25 cm], but twice as thick. It is, however, cooked the same way and will feed six to seven people.

What to look for: The veal eye of round roast is a cylindrical cut that should be the same thickness throughout, except for the tail, which is thinner.

How to cook it: Simply roast this cut in a pan, with 3 to 4 cups [720 to 960 ml] of liquid, to medium (160°F [71°C]). Slice the cooked roast into medallions ¼ to ½ in [6 to 12 mm] and serve.

068

Flank Steak
Veal flank steak is one of the sturdier veal cuts, but it's hard to find because the flank is usually broken down into cutlets. This steak is not as tender as other veal cuts and, consequently, it grills quite nicely.

098

What to look for: You'll need to find a butcher if you want to buy veal flank steak because it's rarely stocked in supermarket meat cases. Look for nearly pure white meat that is at least ½ in [12 mm] thick at its thickest point. A single steak will serve one or two people.

How to cook it: Marinate a flank steak for 1 hour before cooking it. Then grill it over medium-high heat until it is medium (160°F [71°C]). Once it's cooked, let the steak rest for 5 minutes and then slice it against the grain to maintain tenderness.

Hind Shank

The shank is the shinbone. Depending on whom you ask, the famed Italian dish osso bucco is made from either the hind shank or the foreshank. The truth is, you can use either but the hind shank is what the dish was originally created from. It is a less-used muscle than the foreshank, so it is meatier, with more abundant and flavorful marrow (which is considered a delicacy, but it can also be an acquired taste). Many Italian butchers actually call the hind shank "osso bucco."

What to look for: Whether I'm making osso bucco or just braising the cut for a stew, I like to use the hind shank. It's more expensive and you're probably only going to find it at a butcher shop, but it holds together better than the foreshank, and I like the richer marrow. There are only two to three pieces taken out of the center of the hind shank that are right for osso bucco, depending on how thickly they are cut. If the bottom of the piece is a lot wider than the top, there will be more bone than meat on the bottom half of the cut, and the piece won't work as well.

How to cook it: These are bony braising cuts, meant to be cooked for a very long time in ample liquid. The hind shank is usually cut into 2-in [5-cm] pieces for cooking.

099

BEEF

CHUCK **RIB** **LOIN** **ROUND**

BRISKET **PLATE**

As an apprentice butcher working on the chicken table, I would look over in amazement at the experienced butchers rolling out huge sides of beef, marveling as they hung the meat from dangerous-looking hooks. Beef's popularity and the big money it generated meant that the ability to quickly butcher and efficiently break down a side of beef made you a rock star in the industry. A good beef butcher was worth his weight in gold. So when I was told I would have to give up my lunch hour to learn beef, I gladly did.

Unfortunately, things have changed over time, and not for the best. Increasingly, the beef you find in your local supermarket has been cut in industrial operations with more speed and less skill.

But beef remains popular, and for good reason. Even though beef has developed an undeserved reputation for being bad for your health, quality beef is a protein-rich food that is stuffed with valuable nutrients, including the essential vitamins B12, A, E, and D, which is hard to find in many foods. And let's not forget the minerals iron, zinc, selenium, phosphorus, niacin, and riboflavin. So even though beef should not be eaten every day, it still holds an important place in our diets.

"But what about the fat?" people often ask me. Truth be told, beef is not, by its nature, a fatty animal. Unfortunately, back in the '50s, we started feeding corn to our cattle. This made the cattle bigger and fatter, not just under the skin but running through the meat, too. The fat added flavor and weakened the meat fibers, making the meat more tender.

Today, though, the beef you buy has less fat than ever before. A lot less! We're also learning that beef fat, which has long been linked to high cholesterol, may not be the culprit we believed it was. In fact, some of the fats in beef play a neutral or even beneficial role in serum cholesterol. Go figure.

MAKING THE GRADE

American beef can be cut from steers, cows, or bulls. All beef is inspected by the USDA, but only beef from steers is given a USDA grade.

The grade is determined by the amount and saturation of fat (commonly known as **marbling**) in the cut. Fat improves the flavor of meat and keeps it moist during cooking, which is why the greater and more regular the marbling throughout the cut, the higher the grade. The USDA recognizes nine degrees of marbling, from "Traces" to "Very Abundant." Keep in mind, the higher the grade, the higher the price. The following grades are from high to low.

101

Ray's ADVICE

Advertised meat sale prices are used to bring people into the store. This often leads to a high volume of sales for these cuts, increasing turnover and ensuring that you get that cut at its freshest. Take advantage of these sales by buying extra and freezing the meat. That said, not all beef sales are good. Beware of the in-store manager's special, which is a way for operations to clear out meat that is starting to get very close to its expiration date.

 USDA Prime: Marbling from "Moderately Abundant" to "Very Abundant." Prime is the grade of beef served at quality steak houses and restaurants. Only 2 percent of U.S. beef is Prime; it is the best-tasting beef in the world. Whether you roast, braise, or grill the meat, you will taste the difference (and pay dearly for it).

 USDA Choice: Marbling from "Small" to "Moderate." Because of that range, Choice meat can be inconsistent in quality. It's also why, when buying USDA Choice or USDA Select, it is important to inspect the cut itself rather than just go by the grade. A quality Choice cut can often taste as good as a Prime cut. The key with Choice cuts is to cook the meat until it is at least medium-rare. Less marbling results in a chewier piece of meat when cooked rare. Medium-rare is ideal for many cuts to ensure the juices don't evaporate and the flavor is as strong as it can be.

 USDA Select: Cuts with marbling from "Traces" to "Slight." A lack of flavor and a tough texture mark Select cuts. To successfully cook Select meat, slice it very thin or marinate it (or use dry rubs) well in advance of cooking. If you are set on buying a Select steak, go for the rib steak. It has the most fat of any Select cut and will be more flavorful and tender than leaner cuts, like the shell steak (also known as New York strip).

The most common grades in supermarket meat cases are Choice and Select. You'll find USDA Prime cuts at high-end butcher shops.

When I started in the business forty years ago, the standard grade in supermarkets was USDA Choice. Oh, how things have changed. The one-two punch of rising meat costs and increasing customer concern about anything containing fat has pushed most supermarkets to stock the much leaner USDA Select. Remember, when you get rid of the fat, you lose a lot of tenderness and flavor.

Today's USDA Choice isn't the USDA Choice I knew when I was coming up. Before the early 1980s, you could pick up a USDA Choice steak with some really nice marbling. Back then, all kinds of reports started coming out connecting red meat to heart disease. Now, Choice cuts tend to be leaner than they once were. So when someone asks me what grade of steak to buy, I guide them toward USDA Prime if they can find it.

One last thought about grading terms. Any official grade on a package of meat will be preceded by the acronym "USDA." Don't be fooled by marketing terms like "premium" or "extra select." Those mean whatever the seller wants them to mean. Not too long ago, I was at the supermarket with my wife when she picked up a package labeled "premium beef" and "Black Angus." Unfortunately, far below those big bold letters were the words USDA Select. I've been a butcher since long before computers were in every house and a cell phone was in every pocket, but I have no idea what "premium beef" means. So make sure you concern yourself most with whatever comes after USDA.

OTHER BEEF LABEL TERMS

Grass-Fed: This simply means the animal ate grass—as opposed to a less healthful diet of corn or cow feed—right up to the time of slaughter. Grass-fed cattle are much leaner, and their meat is actually darker than meat from grain-fed cattle. Grass-fed beef also has a stronger flavor (some would describe it as slightly gamey, which makes sense because the steers are eating a diet closer to what wild game eat). Grass-fed beef gives you not only the same nutrients that

Ray's ADVICE

The name *Angus* describes a breed of cattle. Once upon a time, that word really meant something, because ranchers were careful about what was and wasn't Angus. Then the Angus Beef Association did a brilliant job of marketing the advantages of the breed, and "Angus" came to mean "quality" in the consumer's mind. That is, until it got watered down to the point that it didn't necessarily mean the best beef you could buy. Today there is Angus, and there is Certified Angus. "Certified" establishes a breed guarantee (which raises the question of what "Angus" alone truly means nowadays) and is consequently higher quality and more expensive.

you find in grain-fed beef but is also leaner and high in omega-3 fatty acids. This means that ground beef, or even beef hot dogs made from grass-fed beef, can be a fantastic way to give kids and adults who don't eat fish a healthy dose of omega-3s.

USDA Organic: This is used on beef that has been fed only USDA Certified Organic grain, grass, or both, and has been cut and packaged in a USDA-certified plant. Nothing touches the meat that is not organic. The meat will carry the distinctive USDA green-and-white logo. Meat packages labeled simply "organic" follow the same guidelines, but if the meat was not butchered in a USDA-certified facility, it cannot carry the official USDA logo. However, it still must conform to organic regulations. That means that beef labeled just "organic" is going to be a lower-priced organic option than a package that carries the USDA Organic shield. For more about organic designation, see page 008.

COOL: This stands for "Country of Origin Labeling" and tells consumers the country in which the beef originated. For more about COOL, see page 010.

104

UNDERSTANDING
SERVING PORTIONS FOR BEEF

Whether you want to pop a roast in the oven or slap some steaks on the grill, here's what you'll need to satisfy two adults and two children. (The general rule of thumb is 4 oz [115 g] of beef per person, but there are some exceptions.)

Boneless or bone-in roast: Any roast must be 2 lb [910 g] or more so it will be thick enough to retain moisture under high-heat roasting. So buy a boneless roast that is at least 2 lb [910 g] for a family of four and plan on having leftovers. Add another 8 to 12 oz [230 to 340 g] for a bone-in roast, to compensate for the weight of the bone.

Chuck roast and brisket: Chuck roast, with its heavy marbling, and brisket, which is very lean, both shrink more than other roasts during cooking, but for different reasons. As the heavy veins of marbling that make up 20 percent of a boneless chuck roast melt, some of the fat is absorbed by the meat but more evaporates, causing the cut to shrink. The brisket has only a fat covering on the bottom, and much of the lean meat is exposed to the heat and loses moisture, causing the piece to shrink. For these cuts, add 1 lb [455 g] to the total you've calculated at 4 oz [115 g] per person, to ensure you have enough meat to go around.

2 steaks, bone-in or boneless, 1 to 1¼ in [2.5 to 3 cm] thick: The thickness guarantees the steaks will cook correctly; and by using two thicker steaks instead of four thinner ones, you shorten the cooking time. That means that the meat holds more flavor; and when sliced, it will feed more people.

1 lb [455 g] ground beef: To make four average-size burgers.

105

Now for my favorite part: Breaking down the meat. In meat-cutting operations, different beef cuts are organized into five very large **primal cuts.** Everyone does this a little bit differently; what I call the **loin** is sometimes broken down even further into the **short loin, sirloin,** and even **tenderloin.**

You'll probably never handle a whole primal—it's certainly not how you buy your meat out of the case—but I've used the primals here as a way of organizing the cuts, from the front of the animal to the back. The most important information for you to know is that some sections of the animal are more tender, while others are less, and the same is true for flavor. So don't worry too much about primals—you'll probably prefer to just scan the meat case for a cut that seems right for the mouths you have to feed, the occasion, and your budget. Whatever the case, the cuts detailed here come from these primals: the **chuck, brisket** and **plate, rib, loin,** and **round.**

Ground Beef (not pictured)

If you take nothing else away from this section, remember this: Not all ground beef is created equal. The best ground beef is ground fresh for you, not preground and packaged. But if you don't have a butcher to turn to, the following guidelines will help you make smart purchases from the case.

What to look for: I've had a lot of customers complain to me that the ground meat they buy is a bright color in the package, but darker on the inside. That's supposed to happen. The meat is only cherry red where it's exposed to air. In fact, you should only be concerned if the ground meat is not darker on the inside. Also, the leaner the meat, the darker it will be on the inside. Buy ground chuck (20 percent fat) if you're making meat loaf or chili. It's fairly lean, but still has some flavor. Look for a coarse grind. The larger grind will make a thicker, richer chili. Go with ground sirloin (10 percent fat) for the grill. This should be your burger meat—don't use ground chuck. The leaner meat from the sirloin is not as reliant on fat for its strong, beefy taste. Whatever ground

106

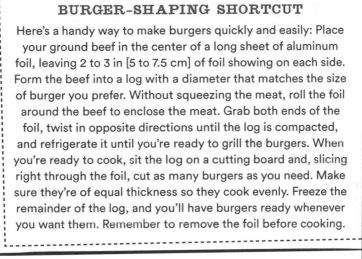

BURGER-SHAPING SHORTCUT

Here's a handy way to make burgers quickly and easily: Place your ground beef in the center of a long sheet of aluminum foil, leaving 2 to 3 in [5 to 7.5 cm] of foil showing on each side. Form the beef into a log with a diameter that matches the size of burger you prefer. Without squeezing the meat, roll the foil around the beef to enclose the meat. Grab both ends of the foil, twist in opposite directions until the log is compacted, and refrigerate it until you're ready to grill the burgers. When you're ready to cook, sit the log on a cutting board and, slicing right through the foil, cut as many burgers as you need. Make sure they're of equal thickness so they cook evenly. Freeze the remainder of the log, and you'll have burgers ready whenever you want them. Remember to remove the foil before cooking.

beef you buy, use it the day you buy it or freeze it right away. Don't let it sit in the refrigerator or the quality, flavor, and freshness will degrade.

How to cook it: Thickness is more important than diameter when it comes to keeping the most flavor inside a burger, where it belongs. Your burgers should never be less than ¾ in [2 cm] and no more than 1¼ in [3 cm] thick. Handmade burgers always have more flavor than premade, machine-processed burgers, which are too thin to stand up to the heat of grill and have had most of the natural juices pressed out of them. Make your patties with nothing but simple seasonings, handle them as little as possible before and during cooking, and you'll be happy with the result. Let burgers sit for a few minutes before serving so that the juices and flavors evenly saturate the meat.

107

Chuck

All chuck cuts are best suited for slow, liquid-based cooking because they come from the front end of the animal, which is the muscular, working end. Although the meat contains nice marbling, it is also tough. The heavy marbling keeps the cuts moist and flavorful during slow cooking, and the slow cooking ensures the meat is not just tender, but fork-tender!

THE SECRET TO THE BEST MEAT LOAF AND MEATBALLS

If you want the freshest, tastiest meat loaf or meatballs possible, you'll want to grind your own chuck. You can use this same process to grind lamb and pork to mix with beef in meatballs or other recipes. You can also use it to grind sirloin for burgers, or lean turkey or chicken. To grind the meat, you will need a grinding assembly for your stand mixer.

1. Cut the chuck into 1½-in [4-cm] cubes.

2. Grinding creates heat that can actually partially cook the meat, so chill the meat in a freezer for 20 to 30 minutes, just so the cubes are hard but not frozen all the way through. Put the grinding assembly from the stand mixer into the freezer with the meat, for the same reason.

3. Begin grinding the cubes, feeding them slowly and steadily into the cold grinder. Grind the meat three times for meatballs or meat loaf and two times for chili.

4. Add spices, garlic, or herbs as desired, mixing them in after the meat is ground to give you better control of the saturation and amounts and to ensure the spices don't gum up the grinder (another reason to chill meat before grinding).

Ray's ADVICE

People regularly ask me the difference between a steak and roast, since the cuts often come from the same primal, or area of the animal. In general, if the cut is 1½ in [4 cm] thick or less, it is labeled as steak; cuts 2 in [5 cm] thick or more are sold as roasts.

Stew Meat (not pictured)

Even though many different cuts of beef are cubed for stew meat, there is only one—stew meat cut from the chuck—that turns stew into a great beef experience. Stew meat cut from the leaner top round will often end up tasteless and chewy.

Stew is a way to utilize less-expensive and less-desirable pieces of meat. The long cooking time and abundant liquid involved in stewing guarantees that even tough beef will be succulent and tender by the time the stew is ready to serve. It's a great way to limit meat portions, slow-cook a dinner while you are at work, and economically feed a family.

109

What to look for: I use the chuck tender for my stew meat because it is one of the leanest parts of the chuck and full of flavor. Stew meat should be cut into 1½-in [4 cm] cubes. Look for chuck cuts on sale to get the best value, and then either cube the meat yourself or have it cubed by the butcher. Buy prepackaged stew meat only if it was packaged that day and the label reads "beef chuck." Move pieces of prepackaged stew meat around in the package with your fingers; many times you will find the meat is strips, not cubes.

How to cook it: Stew meat is always cooked a long time in 3 to 4 cups [720 to 960 ml] of liquid—the staples of any decent stew recipe. You ensure the stew meat comes out fork tender if you use a recipe with an acidic agent, such as red wine or apple cider vinegar, in the base. For me, it isn't stew without a loaf of fresh Italian bread on the table.

First-Cut and Second-Cut Chuck Steaks (also known as First-Cut and Second-Cut Chuck Blade Steaks)

070

First-cut chuck steaks are nicely marbled steaks cut from the rib end of the chuck. These cuts are usually big enough for three or four people. They are more tender and flavorful than the second-cut chuck steaks, which are cut closer to the neck and are leaner.

What to look for: The chuck steak is lighter in color than other steak cuts. The first-cut should be pale red with nice marbling throughout. It will include a flat hunk of the blade bone, and a piece of fat will have been cut out of the middle from one side.

How to cook it: After a good soak in a marinade, chuck steak can be grilled, broiled, or panfried.

Semiboneless Chuck Steak or Roast

071

This is the chuck steak with the blade bone removed and missing the piece of flat iron and chuck tender across the top. It is sold as a steak or roast, depending on its thickness. This cut represents good value for your money because it's cut from the heart, or center, of the neck, without the blade bone and gristle that runs through a flat iron.

What to look for: Chuck meat is a little darker than other cuts, but still a fairly light red. Dark red to purple meat is called dark cutter in the industry; the meat will have a gamier taste and be less tender. A semiboneless roast should be at least 2 in [4 cm] thick.

How to cook it: Chuck roast is best cooked in a slow cooker or Dutch oven with 4 cups [960 ml] or more of liquid, such as vegetable broth. The best way to cook chuck steak is by braising it in an acidic sauce, such as a tomato-based sauce.

110

THE RIGHT STEAK FOR THE OCCASION

The list that follows includes the many steaks that are cut from a steer. It is meant to be an at-a-glance shopping resource; you can learn more about these steaks in the individual listings. The lesser choices here can still be flavorful meals; they just take more work to prepare, tenderize, and cook. If you have your sights set on the best possible steak experience, seek out USDA Prime.

When the night calls for something special: New York Strip Steak, also known as Shell Steak (page 119); Porterhouse (page 120); T-Bone Steak (page 120); Tenderloin, also known as Filet Mignon (page 122); Rib-Eye Steak (page 117); Sirloin Steak (page 121).

When you just want that hearty beef flavor: Hanger Steak, also known as Butcher's Tenderloin (page 124); Skirt Steak (page 116); Flank Steak (page 125); Tri-Tip Roast and Steak (page 126); Culotte Roast and Steak (page 121).

When the beer is more important than the steak: Rib Steak (page 117), Top Round Steak (page 125).

Chuck Roast and Chuck Eye Roast

Most chuck roasts are sold with the bone in, which gives them a better flavor when cooked and helps keep the meat moist as well. There is great value for the money in this cut, which is why it's the most popular one for making pot roast. The great thing about chuck roast is that you don't really have to worry about over-cooking it because the extensive marbling ensures the meat will not dry out.

What to look for: I recommend looking chuck roast in the eye, meaning that you should find a chuck eye roast. The eye is composed of the center three muscles, which resemble a rib-eye steak. The presence of the eye means there is even more marbling. The bigger the eye, and the more marbling, the better the flavor.

How to cook it: Two words come to mind—*slow cooker*. Put a 3½- to 4-lb [1.6- to 1.8-kg] chuck roast into the slow cooker with about 4 cups [960 ml] of water; a generous amount of chopped carrots, potatoes, and onions; and a dose of your favorite spice combination and let it go for 10 to 12 hours on low. When it's done, the meat will fall off the bone and satisfy even the most finicky eater.

Chuck Tender (also known as Mock Tender)

073
This cut comes off the side of the shoulder blade bone, opposite the flat iron steak. It is not as marbled as other chuck cuts, but it is still full of flavor. Don't buy chuck tender when you're pressed for time. Despite the name, tender it isn't. But it can be tenderized by long, slow cooking and will be delicious when cooked. You'll find it economical to begin with, but if it goes on sale at your market, stock up and freeze the extra.

What to look for: This cut is larger on one end, tapering down as it goes, like a filet mignon. It has a thin line of sinew running through the middle, which will be visible only on the face of the larger end. The cut is modest in weight—from 2 to 3 lb [910 g to 1.4 kg].

How to cook it: This is perhaps the best cut for beef stew. Have a butcher cut it up for you, or do it yourself. There will be no need for knives on the table, because it will come out fork-tender if you cook it for hours in a liquid, such as a combination of red wine and beef broth.

Shoulder (also known as Clod, Shoulder Roast, and Shoulder Clod Roast)

074

This cut is rich in flavor, like neck meat, but with less marbling.

What to look for: The shoulder, like other chuck meat, should be light red. Look for a piece with at least moderate marbling.

How to cook it: Because this particular area of the animal gets a good workout and lacks the marbling that would otherwise break up the fibers, the cut should be marinated for about 24 hours before cooking to be well tenderized. It is at its most tender sliced thin.

Chuck Short Ribs

075

These are one of two types of short ribs cut from cows. The other type is cut from the ends of the rib bones. Chuck short ribs are the better of the two. Those cut from the ribs are more common because the ribs themselves are popular, and it's profitable for a market to sell the rib ends as short ribs. Chuck short ribs, on the other hand, are basically a chuck roast with the rib bones left on. Although most supermarket shoppers head right for the pork spareribs when they have a hankering for ribs, beef short ribs are actually a great economical alternative. They require a lot more tenderizing, but you'll save a lot of money and enjoy every bit as much flavor as you would with pork ribs.

What to look for: Chuck short rib bones are usually halved to make 3- to 4-in [7.5- to 10-cm] pieces. There is more meat on one end of the rib than the other, about 1 in [2.5 cm] on one side and 2½ in [6 cm] on the other. The thickest short ribs are sometimes sold on their own and are called an English cut.

How to cook it: The best way to cook short ribs? Braise, braise, and braise some more. The meat will just fall off the bone. However, short ribs are often slow-cooked in true barbecue style, like spareribs, at a temperature of less than 250°F [121°C]. You can also have a butcher remove the meat from the bone for you—it makes incredible stew meat. The cooked meat is so rich in flavor that you only need 1 to 1½ short ribs per person.

076

Flat Iron Steak (also known as Top Blade Steak)

The name of this steak comes from its triangular shape. Its heavy marbling gives it great flavor, but as with all cuts from the chuck, you'll need to tenderize this cut with an acidic marinade or by pounding with a tenderizing mallet.

What to look for: Depending on where you buy your flat iron steak, it may have a streak of gristle running right through the center. You can have a butcher cut the gristle out, or you can make two smaller steaks out of the cut to eliminate the gristle. If there are no flat irons in the case with the gristle already removed, another option is to braise the meat. Braising softens the gristle, making it easy to remove after cooking.

How to cook it: The flat iron steak is a versatile cut, which can be braised, grilled, or panfried. A good long soak in a marinade helps ensure the meat will be tender any way you cook it. I prefer to prepare it like I do other steaks—seasoned simply with salt and pepper. After marinating it, I let it sit at room temperature for 5 to 10 minutes and then panfry it for 4 to 6 minutes per side for medium (160°F [71°C]). Then I let the meat rest for 3 to 5 minutes before serving.

Shoulder Tender (also known as Petite Tender or Bistro Fillet)

You'll have to search for this amazingly tender cut, but when you find it, you'll have struck gold. The shoulder tender is not a common cut, because it takes some experience and skill to extract it. It is similar in texture and fat content to the filet mignon—and just as pricey.

What to look for: You're most likely to find the shoulder tender at a butcher shop because of the skill needed to remove the cut. That also accounts for its premium price. If you find it at a grocery store, it will probably have been cut into medallions, which are just as good for cooking purposes. The shoulder tender should be lighter in color than other shoulder cuts, usually a pale pink.

How to cook it: This cut is vulnerable to overcooking. Do not cook it beyond medium (160°F [71°C]), or you'll have a tough piece of meat. Try coating the meat with a mustard or herb rub and then roasting it in a 350°F [180°C] oven for about 25 minutes for medium-rare.

BRISKET AND PLATE

The brisket and plate is the underside of the belly, which runs from the front of the chest to the loin. You'll find some economical cuts in this area, namely **brisket** and **skirt steak.** Put in the extra effort and time required to cook them right, and they will both provide deep, satisfying flavor.

Brisket (Whole, Point, and Flat)

The brisket owes its popularity and success to the kosher Jewish community and Southern barbecue pitmasters. And since the brisket tends to be tough, it is the largest affordable cut for the holidays. Jewish cooks and others (including early American ranchers) realized it was ideal for heavy spicing and slow cooking. The whole brisket is the first and second cut together. The first cut is the larger and leaner of the two muscles. The point brisket is the

115

thicker side, and the flat cut is the thinner side. The point brisket and flat cut are also sold separately. The flat cut is heavily marbled, and thus more flavorful. Its excessive fat makes it less desirable to most consumers, which is why it is usually inexpensive. The point brisket, being bigger and leaner, is ideal for large gatherings or family get-togethers.

What to look for: Brisket should not be excessively trimmed; it should have a nice cap of fat. Keep in mind that brisket will shrink quite a bit when cooked, so allow 8 oz [230 g] per person when determining the weight you need to buy. Because the cut's popularity peaks around the winter holidays, it is a great value during the rest of the year. Don't hesitate to buy ahead and freeze.

How to cook it: Trim the fat cap (the layer of fat covering the top) down to a thickness of about ⅓ in [8 mm] before cooking. A brisket can be cooked the same way you would cook a pot roast. But it is a classic cut for true low-and-slow barbecuing; hours of cooking under intense smoke at low temperatures yields an incredibly flavorful and tender meat. This is also the cut used to make delectable corned beef and pastrami.

079

Skirt Steak

This thin cut is taken from the diaphragm and can be a tough piece of meat. That's the bad news. The good news is that it has unrivaled marbling, which ensures the meat will brim over with buttery, delicious flavor once cooked. You won't find a better value cut on the cow. If you're willing to marinate the meat and cook it medium-rare, everyone at your table will be begging for more, and you'll be laughing all the way to the bank.

What to look for: Look for outside skirt steak without a lot of extra exterior fat (which you'll pay for and then have to trim), and with the membrane already removed. Dont' try to buy "inside" skirt steak; you will be able to tell the difference by the width. "Outside" skirt steak is only 2 to 3 in [5 to 7.5 cm] wide.

How to cook it: Always remove the skirt steak's membrane if it wasn't removed before sale. Marinate for no more than 1 hour before cooking. The skirt steak absorbs liquid faster than any other cut, and after an hour the marinade will start to cure the meat, ironically making it tougher. Cook over high heat until it is at least medium-rare (145°F [63°C]). The cut cooks quickly, so give it no more than 6 minutes per side. Never serve it whole—skirt steak has to be sliced against the grain (clearly visible as striations on the surface). Otherwise, you'll be chewing it all night. My favorite use for this cut is teriyaki steak. I give it a bath in teriyaki sauce, cut it against the grain into pieces 6 in [15 cm] long, and throw it on the grill.

RIB

The rib primal contains the **rib steak**, **rib-eye steak**, and **rib roast** (also known as **prime rib** or **standing rib roast**). This is the smallest primal and is most often cut into steaks.

Rib Steak and Rib-Eye Steak

As with many cuts that share similar names, the difference here is the bone. The rib steak has one and the rib eye doesn't. Either way, the cut combines a nice light flavor and appealing tenderness because it's taken from a part of the steer that doesn't do much work. As a result, the cut contains the most marbling of any in the animal. The rib eye is basically the trimmed-down heart of the rib steak; you can consider "rib eye" synonymous with "boneless." The USDA describes it as steak or roast trimmed to within 2 in [5 cm] or less of the eye.

What to look for: When shopping for a rib-eye steak, look for a fine texture and light color. Because so much marbling runs through the rib, even a Select grade should show modest marbling. The whiter the outer fat, the better. The eye of the rib starts on the chuck side, where three muscles with a piece of fat in the middle narrow to one muscle on the loin side (also known as the first-cut

080

117

side). Both sides are equally tender and juicy, but the chuck side has a lighter flavor, while the loin side is slightly less juicy but with a stronger flavor. When shopping for a rib roast, the rule of thumb is one rib for every two people.

How to cook it: Rub the meat with a little olive oil before cooking. This will ensure a light outer crust, which will hold in flavor and juices. Sprinkle with sea salt before serving. This cut is also a flavor sponge, which cooks up wonderfully when given an herb-heavy rub or marinade before it hits the heat.

031

Rib Roast (also known as Prime Rib or Standing Rib Roast)

This is the king of roasts. The size and heavy marbling of the prime rib make it perfect for roasting and the ideal choice to feed a large group on the most special of occasions.

What to look for: Just because the label says "prime rib" doesn't mean that what you're getting is the real deal. You have to look for the USDA grade. The rib in any grade is the most marbled cut, but a Select grade prime rib has virtually none of the marbling that makes this such a great cut of meat. Do yourself a favor and buy USDA Choice or Prime. If you can find only USDA Select, you're better off buying filet mignon—a cut that doesn't rely on marbling for its flavor and tenderness. The rule of thumb when estimating portions of prime rib is one rib for every two people.

How to cook it: The goal when cooking rib roast is to get a beautiful, delicious crust on the outside with a lovely, pink medium-rare inside. The best way to achieve both is to coat the outer fat with a thick layer of seasoned rub or kosher salt and massage it into the meat. The total cooking time should come to about 12 minutes per 1 lb [455 g]. Start the meat out in an oven preheated to 475°F [240°C] for the first 15 minutes. Then lower the temperature to 375°F [190°C] and cook to medium-rare (145°F [63°C]). Most important, let the meat sit for 15 to 20 minutes before slicing.

118

LOIN

The loin contains some of the most delectable cuts you can buy. It is composed of two subprimals (although some people treat the two as primals in their own right): the **short loin** and the **bottom sirloin**. The short loin in turn includes the **New York strip steak** (also known as **shell steak**), **T-bone steak, porterhouse, hanger steak** (also known as **butcher's tenderloin**), and the **tenderloin** (also known as **filet mignon**). The sirloin includes the **sirloin steak, culotte roast** and **steak** (also known as **bottom sirloin cap steak**), and the **flank steak.**

New York Strip Steak (also known as Shell Steak)

082

This is one of the best steaks you can buy for sheer flavor and versatility, and it's my personal favorite for the grill. This is where the loin of beef starts, and it's the steak that is left after the filet mignon has been removed from the loin. Shell steak is revered by chefs for its strong, beefy taste, and by home cooks for how easy it is to grill. All you need is a few minutes and high heat.

What to look for: This steak is sold bone-in and boneless; I suggest buying it boneless. The strong flavor remains after the bone has been removed, and you'll be paying only for the meat, which makes the boneless cut a better value.

How to cook it: The trick to grilling a great steak like this is to start with one that is thick enough to stand up to the intense heat. Make sure your shell steak is no less than ¾ in [2 cm] and no more than 1½ in [4 cm] thick. Grill the steak over high heat, 6 to 8 minutes per side, turning only once (with tongs not a fork). After you remove the steak from the heat, let it sit for 10 to 12 minutes so that the flavor and juices saturate the meat.

119

T-Bone Steak

083

This cut is almost a twin to the porterhouse, but the T-bone is considered the king of steaks. The bone helps distribute heat evenly throughout the meat during cooking, and keeps the steak enticingly moist. There are only three or four true T-bone steaks in the loin, so expect to pay for the high quality of what is, to many meat lovers, the quintessential steak.

What to look for: When picking out a T-bone to call your very own, look for ¼ in [6 mm] of outer fat, which should be white and solid (if the outer fat is soft, with a yellow tinge, the steak will be tough and taste slightly off). The piece of fillet under the bone should be lighter red than the meat at the top of the steak, and it should be firm, not soft or mushy.

How to cook it: Cook the T-bone just as you would a New York strip steak, for 6 to 8 minutes per side over high heat, turning only once (with tongs, not a fork). After you remove the steak from the heat, let it sit for 10 to 12 minutes so that the flavor and juices saturate the meat.

Porterhouse

084

The porterhouse encompasses all that is great about the loin. It lies just past the T-bone on the primal and shares many qualities with that great cut. Because of its large size and thickness, it is the perfect steak for two people. Like the T-bone, the porterhouse is a pricey cut but well worth the cost in terms of flavor and serving size. Here's a fun fact about the steak: It got its name from boardinghouses in early-twentieth-century New York, which were referred to as "porterhouses." One of these boardinghouses became famous for its dining room and, particularly, for serving this steak.

What to look for: Always buy a porterhouse that is at least 1 in [2.5 cm] thick to ensure that it doesn't dry out during cooking. The fillet on the bottom of the bone has to be at least 2 in [5 cm] across to be a true porterhouse.

120

How to cook it: Like other high-quality steaks, the porterhouse should be cooked over high heat, usually 12 to 15 minutes per side. Let it sit for 10 minutes after cooking to ensure maximum flavor and juiciness. The porterhouse is traditionally served with the meat removed from the bone and sliced. Then the steak is reassembled on the serving platter for presentation.

Sirloin Steak

085

There are actually two sirloin steaks: the bottom and top. The bottom is the better cut. It is a moderately marbled boneless steak that can easily be cooked to absolute delicious perfection. It also can be had for a very reasonable price and is my cut of choice for London broil, the simple preparation for a thick steak or roast that is grilled and then sliced against the grain, on the diagonal. The steak is named for its position in the sirloin primal area at the base of the back.

What to look for: The fat on the outside of the sirloin steak should be white and solid. The meat itself should be slightly lighter in color than either the T-bone or shell steak. The marbling should be light to moderate.

How to cook it: Sirloin steaks are ideal for grilling, as long as you leave enough time to cook it. Grill a 1½-in [4-cm] steak for 10 to 12 minutes per side. Let it sit for 10 minutes before slicing, and then slice the meat at an angle against the grain.

Culotte Roast and Steak (also known as Bottom Sirloin Cap Steak)

086

The culotte is the cap over the sirloin steak. It is the most marbled piece of the sirloin, making it also the most tender. The culotte can be a great London broil because it is tender on its own, while all other London broil cuts—such as the top round and even the flank steak—need to be marinated for tenderness. The culotte is a great choice when you're looking to serve only two or three people.

121

What to look for: This cut looks a bit like a tri-tip because it is triangular. The meat should be a rich red and have a light cover of fat across the top, with just a bit of marbling throughout. Keep in mind that this is a smaller cut; if the meat is more than 2 lb [910 g], it's not a culotte.

How to cook it: The strong sirloin flavor makes a culotte steak perfect for the grill. You can marinate the meat or just rub it with a drizzle of olive oil to create a sear on the outside that traps all the gorgeous flavor inside. Grill it over medium-high heat for 5 to 7 minutes per side. You can also grill, or broil, the roast. In either case, always slice a culotte thin and against the grain.

087

Tenderloin (also known as Filet Mignon)
This is one of the most desirable cuts on a steer because it can be cut into so many fine pieces of meat. The tapered ends of an untrimmed tenderloin can be cut off to use as stew meat or kabobs.

The center of the tenderloin, known as the chateaubriand, is prepared as a roast and is considered one of the best. The tenderloin is also cut into filet mignon steaks. The filet mignon is muscle that does not get used and is therefore incredibly soft and tender, but because it lacks marbling it is not a very flavorful cut. Taken from the loin in one piece, it is considered a luxury cut. But to achieve deliciousness with a filet mignon you must rely on flavoring agents, such as sauces.

What to look for: Tenderloin roast is sold trimmed and untrimmed (for most shoppers, trimmed is preferable). Look for one about 5 lb [2.3 kg], which is an indication that it has been trimmed; untrimmed tenderloin roasts can run 9 lb [4 kg]. Either way, the tenderloin will probably be covered with the silverskin, or membrane. If you don't want to remove it yourself, ask the butcher to remove it for you.

When buying filet mignon, look for an even cherry color across the cut. The steak should look a bit moist in the package (if it's kept too long, it tends to dry out), and it should be firm to the touch. With this cut, in particular, it's very important that the plastic over the package be tightly sealed, because the meat will degrade quickly when in direct contact with oxygen.

How to cook it: The tenderloin is one of the most expensive cuts, but the high price buys you one of the leanest, most tender, and most versatile pieces of meat available. It can be roasted, grilled, or panfried. But first you will need to remove the silverskin. At the large end of the tenderloin, slip a thin blade, such as the blade of a boning knife, just under the membrane. Angle the blade up slightly against the skin, being careful not to cut through, and run the blade from one end of the tenderloin to the other in one motion, literally skinning the membrane off the surface of the meat.

123

To cook a tenderloin roast, fold the tail end under so that the whole roast is the same thickness. Secure it with one or two pieces of kitchen twine (a butcher will gladly do this for you). The roast will cook more evenly, and the meat will adhere to itself so that it can be sliced as one piece after it's cooked, giving you even slices through-out. The filet mignon steak, on the other hand, cooks quickly and goes from done to overdone in a blink. Grill it over high heat for 3 to 5 minutes per side. Given how soft the beef is in this cut, it's import-ant to plan for carry-over cooking—the cooking that continues after the meat is removed from the heat source. So if you want the fillet done medium (160°F [71°C]), remove it from the heat when it is medium-rare (145°F [63°C]). By the time you serve it, it will have continued to cook and will be medium. Serve it—at the very least—with a big pat of herbed butter. Better still, serve it with a rich sauce, such as a bordelaise or a brandy-and-butter brown sauce.

Hanger Steak (also known as Butcher's Tenderloin)

088

This cut hangs from the beef tenderloin (filet mignon) and has an unusual shape—pointed and thinner at one end. The hanger steak is packed with a deep, strong flavor and is extremely juicy. Even though there is only one per animal, the cut remains inexpensive because most people don't know about it. That's partly because the hanger steak has an unappealing look, and many shoppers buy meat with their eyes. I can tell you that butchers have always known how flavorful it is and would take this home themselves when it was left in the meat case at the end of the day. That's why it is known as the butcher's tenderloin.

124

What to look for: A hanger steak is dark red. If you see a large sinew running through it, do not buy it; it should have been removed. No credible meat operation would put them out that way because it takes professional skill to remove the sinew without destroying the steak.

How to cook it: Never cook a hanger steak past medium, but don't serve it rare, either; the meat has a coarse texture. For the same reason, cut it against the grain to ensure the meat is as tender as possible.

Flank Steak

The flank steak has to be marinated for a long time to saturate it with flavor and tenderize it. The cut is 4 to 5 in [10 to 12 cm] wide, 10 in [25 cm] long, and ½ to ¾ in [12 mm to 2 cm] thick. Although it has slight to moderate marbling and a nice flavor, flank steak is famous for its toughness. Cook it right, though, and you'll have a delicious meal.

What to look for: When picking out a flank steak, look for a light red color, which indicates more marbling throughout the meat. That translates to a softer steak, which will absorb a marinade better.

How to cook it: Flank steak is best broiled or grilled. Marinate the meat for about 24 hours and then cook it 6 to 8 minutes per side. Slice the meat thin, at a slight angle against the grain.

ROUND

The round is the back leg and is the leanest part of the animal. This primal contains the most popular cuts for roasts and London broils, not to mention the best cuts and bones for making stocks or soups. The primal consists of the **top round, top sirloin, tri-tip roast and steak** (also known as **Santa Maria roast**), **eye round** (also known as **eye of round roast**), **bottom round** (also known as **rump roast** and **bottom round roast**), and **hind shank** and **marrow bones.**

125

Top Round

This cut is from the inside of the top of the rear leg, and there's no getting around the fact that it has a tendency to be tough. But it has a nice beefy flavor that makes the cut versatile and a favorite for London broil, sandwich steaks, stir-fried beef, and thinly sliced roast beef, which you'll find in the best delis. The big benefit is that this is one of the most inexpensive and leanest cuts you can buy.

What to look for: Top round is one of the most common items in supermarket meat cases. It's one of the leanest beef cuts, so expect to find very minimal marbling and bright pink color. Buy it when-ever it's on sale and freeze it.

How to cook it: Marinate top round for about 24 hours, to give the marinade a chance to penetrate the meat. You'll want to braise the roast and then slice it very thin for sandwiches or for dishes such as involtini.

Top Sirloin

091

Top sirloin has a stronger flavor than top round. But like top round, this cut is dense, fairly tough, and needs to be sliced thin for tenderness. This is a smaller cut than top round, but still good for London broils and roasts, and it is my cut of choice for kabobs. It will also produce the leanest and most flavorful ground beef you will ever have.

What to look for: Look for top sirloin that is 90 percent lean.

How to cook it: Top sirloin is most often cooked as London broil (see above). While the sirloin steak comes from the bottom sirloin and is a good grilling cut, this cut is not as suitable for grilling. To cook it as a steak, panfry for 3 to 4 minutes per side. Let it rest for 10 minutes and slice thinly against the grain.

Tri-Tip Roast and Steak (also known as Santa Maria Roast)

092

Named for its triangular shape with its three tips, tri-tip roast is cut from the top sirloin cap and is exceedingly tender. It is very flavorful and well marbled. The roast is often cut into 1-in- [2.5-cm-] thick tri-tip steaks.

126

What to look for: If you live on the West Coast, your butcher may know this cut as Santa Maria roast. Whatever the roast and steaks are called, you're more likely to them find at a butcher shop or high-end grocery store than in the meat case of a large chain supermarket.

How to cook it: Tri-tip steaks are best broiled after being marinated for several hours. The tri-tip roast should be oven roasted at 450°F [230°C] for about 30 minutes, at which point the roast should be medium-rare (145°F [63°C]).

093

Eye Round (also known as Eye of Round Roast)

This log-shaped cut contains very lean meat. The roast is inexpensive and, when cooked right, can be coaxed to delicious juiciness.

What to look for: Shopping for the perfect eye round is a straightforward affair. Look for fat covering one-quarter of the cut or more, if possible. With this particular cut, leaner is not better.

How to cook it: Here's how I'd suggest you soften up the tough nature of eye round. Salt the roast all over and refrigerate for 1 day. When you're ready to cook, rinse off the salt coating and rub the roast all over with a mixture of olive oil, kosher salt, freshly ground black pepper, minced garlic, and chopped fresh rosemary. Add a special element to the roast by wrapping it in paper-thin slices of beef suet (ask your butcher to cut them) before cooking. Cook the roast in a 475°F [240°C] oven for 25 minutes. Turn off the oven and leave the roast in for 3 hours. Slice thin and serve!

094

Bottom Round (also known as Rump Roast and Bottom Round Roast)

This boneless cut is very lean and dense. It is the toughest of all roasts, but it has good flavor despite a lack of fat. It is thicker on one side than on the other side. The thicker side, closest to the hip bone, is sometimes sold on its own as rump roast; the more tapered side is sold as bottom round roast. Bottom round is best suited for stew meat, but it can make a wonderful corned beef, and it is also used for pot roast.

What to look for: The fat covering on this cut is your indicator of how fresh and well prepared the meat is. Look for fat that is white and solid, and avoid any cut with yellow or soft fat.

How to cook it: There's a very simple formula for cooking a bottom round roast or a rump roast as it should be: a long cooking time (hours and hours) plus low heat (275°F [135°C]), plus at least 4 cups [960 ml] of liquid.

127

095

Hind Shank and Marrow Bones

The hind shank and other marrow bones come from the round. They are rarely used by home cooks these days, and that's a real shame. Cook them right, and you are taking advantage of an incredibly economical way to enjoy great flavor and nutrition.

The hind shank is a well-muscled area that requires long, moist, and penetrating cooking. For that reason, it is almost always used for stocks and soups.

The large bones that run through the round and the hind shank have tons of nutritious beef marrow in them. Cook soup from these bones, and you can feed a lot of people a healthful meal without actually buying a lot of beef.

What to look for: Look for the hind shank with the bone in. The bone will assure you that you're actually getting a hind shank and not a less-desirable foreshank, and it will add flavor to whatever you're cooking.

How to cook it: Add the hind shank, whole or cut into rounds, or marrow bones to a soup and cook in the slow cooker for about 10 hours.

128

APPENDICES

Grilling Basics

Cooking meat and poultry over an open flame is one of the most widely misunderstood ways to cook. Improper grilling has ruined a lot of good meat.

Let's start with the difference between grilling, barbecuing, and smoking. Grilling involves cooking relatively thin cuts, or delicate proteins like chicken, directly over a hot fire (350°F [180°C] or higher) very quickly. True barbecuing is done low and slow—over heat that may fall below 250°F [120°C] for cooking times that can range from 1 hour to more than 12 hours. Barbecued meat is also cooked indirectly, with the heat source off to the side. Although wood smoke flavors barbecue, true smoking involves cooking or curing meat, poultry, or fish with wood smoke—a process that requires a smoker with a separate firebox and lots and lots of time (and fruitwood). Smoking is done at temperatures that are lower than for barbecuing, usually below 200°F [95°C].

Regardless of how you cook the meat you buy, the fuel source will affect the taste of anything that comes off your grill. Charcoal adds a typical cookout flavor that many people love (unless the charcoal is impregnated with fire starter, which I do not recommend using), while gas adds no real flavor. You can add a bit of fruitwood flavor to your cookout specialties by using wood chips. Soak them in water, put them in an aluminum-foil packet, punch holes in the packet, and place it right on the coals or gas burners.

True barbecuing takes a fair amount of expertise, because the heat source has to be kept at a low and steady temperature throughout the process. Low temperatures are difficult to maintain with gas burners. That translates to watching whatever it is you're

129

cooking very closely and keeping the fuel source constant. There are plenty of books that detail how to barbecue like the pros, and they are the best sources for in-depth instructions.

Most people will opt for the quicker, easier method of grilling. No matter what you're grilling, create two or three heat zones by either adjusting the burners on your gas grill or mounding charcoal to different heights under the grate. This allows you to control the cooking time by moving things around on the grill. It's a great way to ensure that your burgers and chicken thighs come off the grill at roughly the same time without either one being dried out.

Make sure you know how to operate your grill correctly. Closing the lid, vents, or both on your grill is how you control the temperature (along with the burner controls on a gas grill). No matter what type of grill you use, you must use a thermometer to monitor the internal temperature of the grill if you're going to cook accurately and get the best results. Many grills have a thermometer built right into the lid, but you want one that shows actual ambient temperatures, not just zones. Just as you would in the kitchen, you should also check the internal temperature of any meat you cook on the grill with an instant-read thermometer.

TOOLS

A good set of grilling tools can make cooking on the grill easier, and it can also ensure that what you take off the grill makes it to the table in good shape. The big secret? Leave the forks in the kitchen. Piercing a piece of meat or poultry with a fork in order to turn it is a sure way to lose precious juices and flavor before you get the meat to the table. The only utensils you'll need for your grilled meat are a heavy-duty spatula and a strong, sturdy pair of outdoor tongs. I use stainless-steel grill tools with wooden handles, which don't conduct heat. Turn burgers with a spatula, and turn them only once. Turn larger cuts with tongs. Another big crime I see grillers commit is pressing the burgers. I don't know why people do this—it's just squeezing flavor and moisture out of the burger.

MARINADES, RUBS, AND SAUCES

The primary reason for using marinades or rubs is to tenderize meat or keep it moist during cooking. Added flavor is a secondary benefit. Sauces are more about adding a splash of flavor, and barbecue sauces should only be added right before the meat is done cooking. They usually have a lot of sugar, which can caramelize and burn if the sauce is left on the meat throughout the cooking process.

You can experiment with your own creations, or you'll find a wealth of recipes for marinades, rubs, and sauces in cookbooks and online. Just keep in mind that you don't want to disguise the meat or poultry's flavor. High-quality cuts like T-bone steak, chicken thighs, or veal loin really need nothing more than a light coating of olive oil and a sprinkle of salt and pepper before they go on the grill.

131

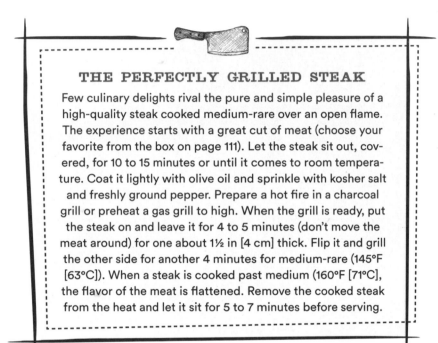

THE PERFECTLY GRILLED STEAK

Few culinary delights rival the pure and simple pleasure of a high-quality steak cooked medium-rare over an open flame. The experience starts with a great cut of meat (choose your favorite from the box on page 111). Let the steak sit out, covered, for 10 to 15 minutes or until it comes to room temperature. Coat it lightly with olive oil and sprinkle with kosher salt and freshly ground pepper. Prepare a hot fire in a charcoal grill or preheat a gas grill to high. When the grill is ready, put the steak on and leave it for 4 to 5 minutes (don't move the meat around) for one about 1½ in [4 cm] thick. Flip it and grill the other side for another 4 minutes for medium-rare (145°F [63°C]). When a steak is cooked past medium (160°F [71°C], the flavor of the meat is flattened. Remove the cooked steak from the heat and let it sit for 5 to 7 minutes before serving.

Cutting a Chicken into Halves and Quarters

If cooking a whole chicken doesn't appeal to you, you can buy a whole roaster and cut it into halves and quarters, which will be perfect for grilling. You will still be getting a great value. You're going to need a sharp 6- to 7-in [15- to 17-cm] boning knife and a large cutting board. Make sure the surface of the cutting board and your hands are clean and dry; wet or slippery surfaces are a recipe for injury. Keep a slightly damp cloth nearby, to wipe your hands and the cutting board as you work.

1. Lay the whole chicken on the cutting board, breast-side up. The neck should be at the top of the cutting board. Use the top 1 in [2.5 cm] of your knife to cut between one leg and the body, opening the joint between the thigh and the back. Do this without cutting completely through the meat. Repeat with the other leg.

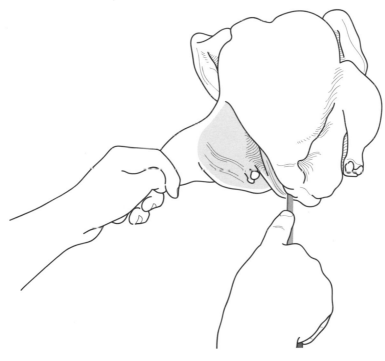

cont'd

2. Turn the chicken over so that the breast side is down and the tail of the chicken is at the top of the cutting board. Place the top 1 in [2.5 cm] of your knife right where the thighbone separates from the back. Grab the tail with one hand and pull toward you while cutting down toward the neck, angling toward the center and into the *V* at the neck (otherwise you'll be trying to slice through rib bones and won't be successful). Repeat on the other side. The back and neck should come out easily in one piece.

134

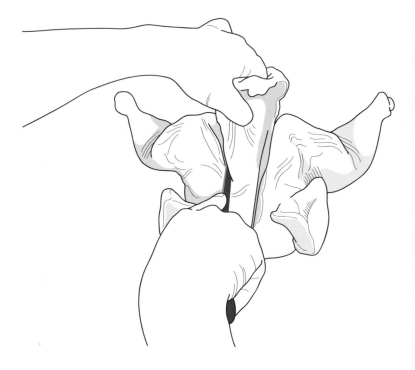

3. Now place the chicken breast-side down and work from the inside out. Push out on the edges of the rib cage, and push the middle of the breast up from underneath to snap the breastbone and force the keel bone (a curved bone that is dark on top and turns to softer white cartilage as it narrows to a point) to pop out at the top. Trace the keel bone with your knife point. This should break the membrane, and the bone will pull out easily.

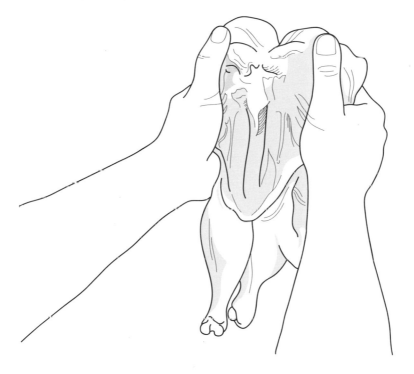

135

cont'd

4. Cut right down the middle to halve the chicken. Cut cleanly through the skin between the thighs and the breast to quarter the chicken.

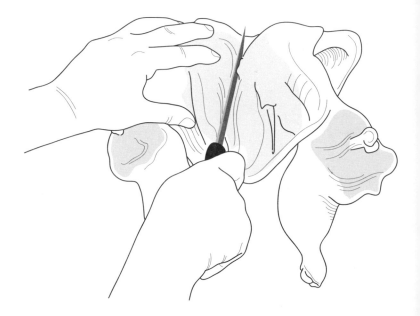

136

How to Carve a Thanksgiving Turkey

Remove the turkey from the oven and let it rest for 20 to 30 minutes before carving. This will give the juices and flavors time to saturate the meat and allow the meat to become cool enough to handle. It's much easier to work on a slightly cooled turkey.

Start the carving process by setting yourself up for success. Make sure you have a spacious, clean, and dry work surface. You'll also need a 6- to 8-in [15- to 20-cm] boning knife, but you will not need a fork. When carving, never use a fork—use your hand instead to prevent any juices from running out.

The big mistake most people make is trying to slice meat right off the bird. Turkey bones are curved, which means you'll inevitably leave a lot of meat on the bones, you won't be able to slice against the grain for tenderness, and the slices will be irregular. The secret is to remove each part of the turkey before you slice it correctly and safely on a cutting board.

1. Start with the whole leg (leg and thigh). Slowly cut through the joint between the body and leg, using the tip of your knife. Apply steady pressure to force the whole leg away from the body, and open up the joint as you cut. Keep cutting until you get to the joint, then cut through the seam of the joint (don't try to cut through the bone—you won't be able to do it).

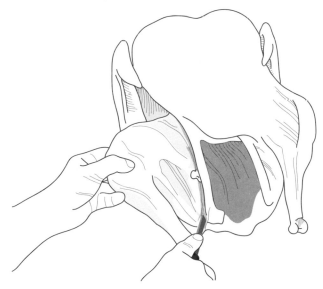

137

cont'd

2. Remove the whole leg, and cut through the joint between the thigh and the drumstick. Use the same process you did in separating the whole leg from the body. Set the drumstick on the platter and repeat with the other whole leg.

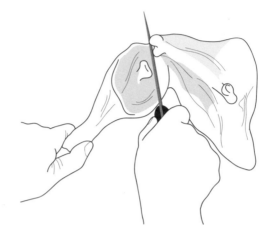

3. Debone the thigh by running the knife along the bone on one side just enough to clearly see the bone. Grab one end of the bone and repeat the process on the other side, turning the bone as you cut. The bone should roll right out.

138

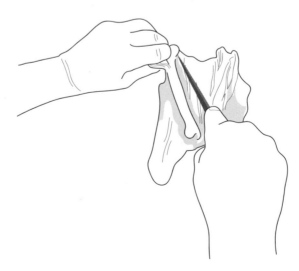

4. Cut the thigh into thick slices and arrange on the platter between the drumsticks.

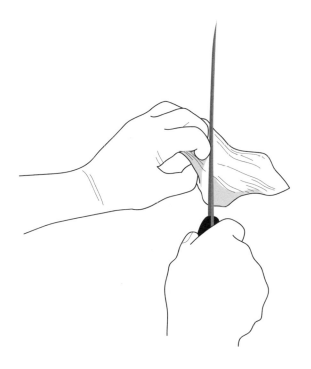

cont'd

139

5. Cut off the wing by grabbing the tip and pulling the wing out. Cut through the joint at the bottom of the *V* of the wing. This will leave the drumette connected to the body, making the bird more stable and preventing it from rolling when you remove the breast meat. The drumettes can easily be removed at the end of the carving process. Repeat with the opposite wing and arrange the wings on either side at the front of the serving platter.

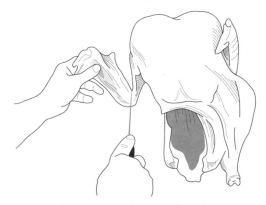

6. Remove the breast meat by running the point of the knife along one side just under the top of the bone where the meat attaches. Cut front to back, scoring the bone and creating an opening just big enough to slide your fingertips between the meat and bone. Pull the meat away from the bone steadily and evenly as you run the point of your knife along the curve of the bone.

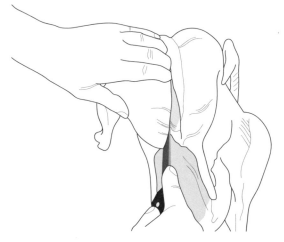

140

7. On a cutting board, slice the breast meat at least ¼ in [6 mm] thick, to keep the slices from drying out when they come in contact with the air. Cut against the grain. (Determine the direction of the muscle fibers, and cut perpendicular to those lines in the meat.) This will ensure the slices are solid and hold together, and, most important, that they remain tender. Arrange the slices down the center of the platter by laying them down straight across between the wings, shingling them as you go. This will ensure that less of the meat is exposed to air, so that the slices will be kept moist and warm.

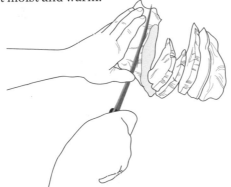

8. After you've removed the breast, trace the wishbone that runs along the top of the breast by the neck with the point of your knife. The wishbone will pull out easily and cleanly.

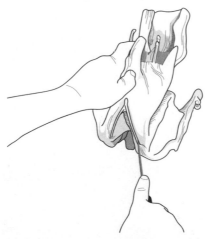

cont'd

9. Remove the drumettes by pulling them away from the body to expose the joint and running a knife through the joint.

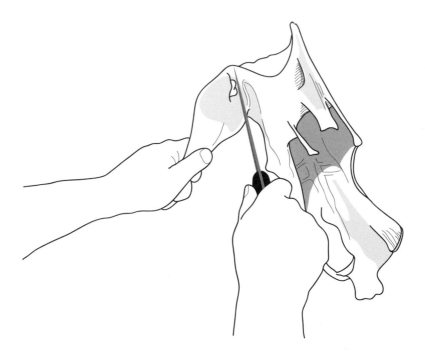

142

How to Tie a Roast

Tying a roast is a fairly basic and simple kitchen technique, which is used to maintain the appearance of the roast and to secure a folded or stuffed roast so that it cooks evenly and correctly. Meat can expand and swell as it cooks, so tying keeps a roast in a pleasingly uniform shape for presentation and slicing.

The key is to tie the roast only tight enough to hold it together. Tie it too tight or use too many strings, and you'll lose the natural juices as the meat expands and the strings squeeze juices out of the roast. That will leave you with a dry and flavorless roast. Here's how to tie any roast.

1. Starting at one end of the roast, run a piece of kitchen string underneath the roast, and back up to meet over the top.

2. Hold the two ends of string side by side. With the index and second fingers of your other hand, pull the short piece down and give one twist to create a loop. Bring the loop up on the other side of the long string. Pull the tail from the loop over the top of the longer piece and through the loop, and pull to tighten. (You just created a **butcher's slipknot**.)

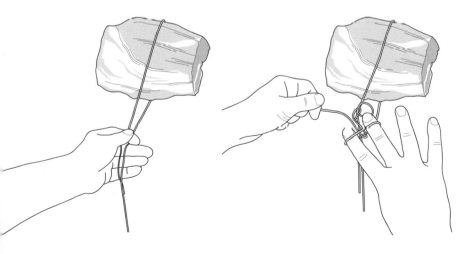

143

cont'd

3. Pull the longer piece of string up and slide the knot down until it rests snugly against the roast. Tie a regular knot to hold the slipknot in place. Cut off any excess string just past the knot.

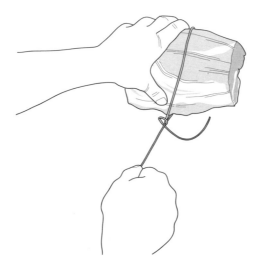

144

4. Repeat three or four times along the length of the roast, positioning the loops 1 in [2.5 cm] apart for stuffed roasts and 2 to 3 in [5 to 7.5 cm] apart for solid roasts.

POULTRY

001 Whole Chicken

002 Whole Turkey

003 Whole Leg
(also known as Airline Cut)

004 Drumstick

005 **Thigh** [clockwise from top left: skin on, skinless, top side, and bottom side]

006 **Breast**
[left to right: split and whole]

007 **Cutlets** [clockwise from top: sliced and pounded, tenders, and whole]

008 **Wings**

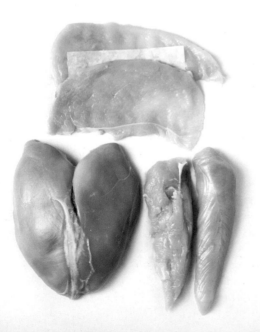

009 Picnic Roast
(also known as Pork Picnic Shoulder or Cali)

010 Shoulder Butt
(also known as Boston Butt)

PORK

011 Pork Neck Bones

012 Rib End Roast

013 Rib Blade Chops
(also known as Rib End Chops)

014 Country-Style Spareribs

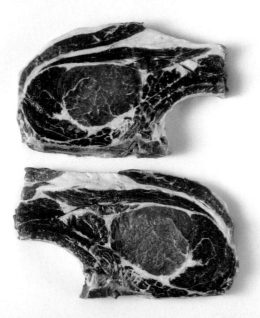

015 Pork Loin Roast
(also known as Center Loin Roast)

016 Pork Crown Roast

017 Center-Cut Pork Chops
[left to right: bone-in and boneless]

018 Tenderloin

019 Sirloin Roast
(also known as Loin End Roast)

020 Pork Sirloin Chops
(also known as Loin End Chops)

021 Pork Cutlets

022 Baby Back Ribs

023 Spareribs

024 Pork Belly (Whole)

025(a) Salt Pork

025(b) Bacon

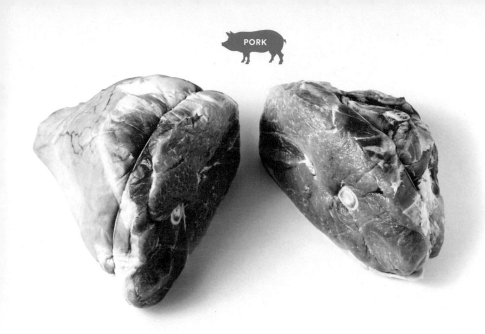

026 Leg (also known as Fresh Ham)
[left to right: shank half and butt half]

027 Smoked Ham
[left to right: shank half and butt half]

PORK

028 Shank Roast
(also known as Ham Shank)

029 Ham Hock
(also known as Pork Knuckle)

030 Smoked Shank

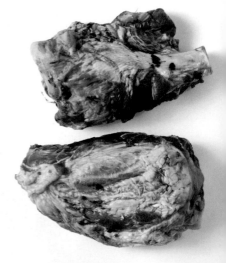

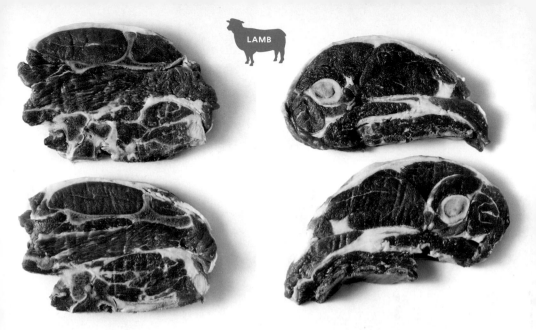

LAMB

031 Shoulder Blade Chops
(also known as Shoulder Chops)

032 Shoulder Arm Chops
(also known as Round Bone Chops)

033 Shoulder Roast

034 Foreshank
(also known as Lamb Shank)

035 Lamb Neck

036 Rib Chops

LAMB

037 Rack of Lamb

038 Crown Roast

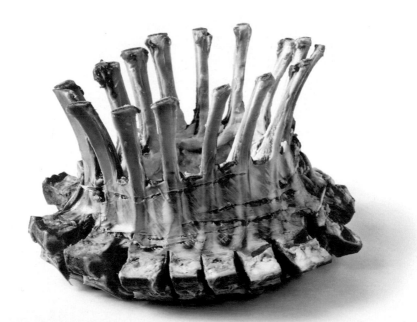

LAMB

039 Breast

040 Riblets

041 Loin Chops

LAMB

042 Loin Roast

043 Lamb Tenderloin

LAMB

044 Leg of Lamb

045 Shank Half Leg

046 Butt Half Leg

047 Butterflied Leg

048 Sirloin Chops

049 Sirloin Roast

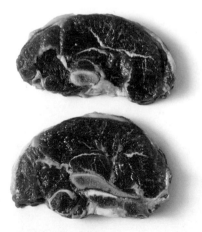

LAMB

050 Leg Steak

051 Cutlets

052 Shoulder Chops
(also known as Shoulder Blade Chops)

053 Round Bone Chops

VEAL

VEAL

054 Shoulder Roast
(also known as Clod Roast)

055 Shoulder Cutlets

056 Chuck Roast

057 Breast [left] **and Brisket** [right]

058 Rib Chops

059 Rack of Veal

VEAL

060 Rib-Eye Roast
(also known as Veal Fillet)

061 Strip Loin

062 Porterhouse
(also known as Loin Chops)

VEAL

063 Tenderloin Roast [left] **and Medallions** [right]

064 Sirloin Roast
(also known as Veal Rump Roast)

065 Leg Cutlets

066 Scaloppine

067 Top Round

068 Flank Steak

069 Hind Shank

BEEF

070 First-Cut and Second-Cut Chuck Steaks
(also known as First-Cut and Second-Cut Chuck
Blade Steaks)

071 Semiboneless Chuck Steak or Roast

072 Chuck Roast and Chuck Eye Roast

073 Chuck Tender (also known as Mock Tender)
[left to right: sliced chuck tender and whole]

BEEF

074 Shoulder (also known as Clod,
Shoulder Roast, and Shoulder Clod Roast)

075 Chuck Short Ribs

076 Flat Iron Steak (also known as Top Blade
Steak) [left to right: steaks and whole roast]

BEEF

077 Shoulder Tender
(also known as Petite Tender or Bistro Fillet)

078 Brisket (Whole, Point, and Flat)

079 Skirt Steak

080 Rib Steak [left] and Rib-Eye Steak [right]

BEEF

081 Rib Roast
(also known as Prime Rib or Standing Rib Roast)

082 New York Strip Steak
(also known as Shell Steak)

083 T-Bone Steak

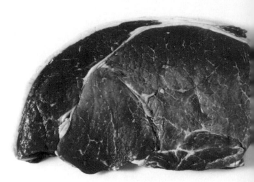

BEEF

084 Porterhouse

085 Sirloin Steak

086 Culotte Roast and Steak
(also known as Bottom Sirloin Cap Steak)

087 Tenderloin (also known as Filet Mignon)
[left to right: whole tenderloin and filets mignons]

088 Hanger Steak
(also known as Butcher's Tenderloin)

089 Flank Steak

090 Top Round

091 Top Sirloin

BEEF

092 Tri-Tip Roast and Steak
(also known as Santa Maria Roast)

093 Eye Round
(also known as Eye of Round Roast)

094 Bottom Round (also known as
Rump Roast and Bottom Round Roast)

095 Hind Shank and Marrow Bones

INDEX

177

178

179

180

181

182

183

184